The Step-By-Step

NUWAVE

AIR FRYER

COOKBOOK

220 DELICIOUS AND EASY RECIPES FOR BEGINNERS

CANDICE HEATH

CONTENTS

APPETIZERS AND SNACKS 46

INTRODUCTION

How do NuWave Air Fryer Works?

Air fryers work by circulating hot air around the food in a very similar way to convection ovens. A heating element inside the air fryer distributes hot air through a fan so that it's pushed around the food in circular motions. This way of cooking food is actually quicker than traditional methods because the heat is evenly distributed around the food. If you're cooking frozen fries in an air fryer, you can expect this to take around 15 minutes.

While air-frying might not be quite as fast as deep-frying, you'll be using significantly less oil, and you won't need to blot your food onto a paper kitchen towel. Most air fryers have removable baskets in which you place your food, and these have small holes all around their edges that allow the hot air to reach the food inside. In order for the air to circulate effectively though, you'll need to make sure you're not overfilling the basket so that the hot air can reach all sides of the food. Air fryer baskets sit pretty snugly against the sides of the appliance, ensuring that minimal heat is lost during cooking.

What Are the Benefits of NuWave Air Fryer?

I'm sure you have seen the online buzz about air fryers! These appliances are definitely the most popular and trendy thing happening in the kitchen this year. Maybe you are curious about what all the hype is about? When I first heard about them, I was curious as well. Why ARE people so excited about these things? I love some good fries as much as the next person, but can one unit really do more than that? How can frying anything be healthy?

These appliances are not a fryer in the same way that a deep-fat fryer is. They are more like a small, self-contained convection oven. They use electrical elements to quickly heat the air, and then circulate this hot air around and through your food. This hot air cooks the food quickly, so crispy things get browned but the inside stays moist and delicious. Here are some benefits of cooking with an air fryer:

1. Healthier Cooking

So, how can frying something be healthy? Easy! These appliances can be used without any oil at all, or with just a tiny spritz of oil if you choose to use it. You can cook frozen fries, onion rings, wings and more, and still get really crispy results without the extra oil. Compared to using my oven, the fries from the air fryer were crispier but not dried out, and using it to make breaded zucchini wedges was even more impressive!

2. Quicker Meals

Since they are smaller than an oven and circulate the air around with fans, they cook foods faster as well. An oven can take up to 20-30 minutes to properly preheat, whereas these fryers come to the temperature within minutes. I was really impressed that my frozen fries were perfect after 15 minutes when they take up to 45 minutes in the oven. If you need to make snacks or meals in a hurry, you will probably love this time saver.

3. Versatility

I think this is my favorite feature of an air fryer. You can do SO MUCH with it! Yes, it fries really well compared to an oven. But it also can bake (even cakes), broil, roast, grill and stir fry! Feel like chicken and snow peas for dinner? Easy to make with one of these.

You can cook fresh and frozen foods and even reheat leftovers in them. I have done meats, fish, casseroles, sandwiches and a lot of different veggies in mine. Some fryers come with extra features, like a rotisserie rack, grill pan or elevated cooking rack. Dividable baskets mean you can cook several things at the same time as well. It is impressive that a single unit can cook so many things in so many ways.

Depending on the size of your fryer, there are a lot of different accessories you can buy. Cake and pizza pans, kabob skewers and steamer inserts are just a few of the accessories I have seen available. There are many recipe books for sale, and online recipes are easy to find too.

4. Space Saver

If you have a small kitchen, or live in a dorm room or shared housing, you might appreciate this benefit. Most of these units are about the size of a coffee maker. They don't take up too much room on the counter, and they are usually easy to store away or move. I appreciate the fact that they can replace other appliances like a toaster oven, and some folks use them in kitchenettes or RVs that lack a real oven. They are very handy to have in an office break room too!

5. Ease of Use

Most fryers are really easy to use- just select the temperature and the cooking time, add food and shake a few times while cooking. No need to fuss or stir like using the stove top.

The baskets make shaking your food simple and fast as well, and the unit doesn't lose a lot of heat when you open it. So feel free to peek while cooking if you want! Unlike an oven, you won't be slowing things down if you do.

6. Ease of Clean Up

One part of cooking that most of us don't enjoy is the clean up. With an air fryer, you just have a basket and pan to clean, and many are even dishwasher safe. With non-stick coated parts, food usually isn't stuck to the pan and instead slides right off onto your plate. It takes just a few minutes to wash up after using. This inspires me to cook at home more often because I don't dread the clean up!

7. Energy Efficiency

These fryers are more efficient that using an oven, and they won't heat up you house either. I've been using mine during a heat wave, and I love that my kitchen isn't hot while I'm using it. If you are trying to keep your house cool during the summer, or are worried about your electric bill, then you will be impressed with how efficient these units are.

How to Use NuWave Air Fryer?

Here are a few more tips for getting the most out of your air fryer:

1. Adjust the Cooking Temperature

When converting a recipe with a suggested temperature for deep-frying or cooking in a traditional oven, lower the air fryer's temperature by 25°F to achieve similar results. So if a recipe calls for deep-frying chicken in oil heated to 350°F, air fry at 325°F. The same rule applies for converting roasting recipes. This adjustment is needed because the circulating air makes the heat of the cooking environment more consistent, and thus more intense than traditional cooking methods. Remember to pre-heat your air fryer to temperature—it usually takes less than 5 minutes—before filling the basket, just as you would with any other cooking method.

2. Toss Ingredients With Oil, Sparingly

In general, you should toss food with one to two tablespoons of oil (whichever kind you like: olive, coconut, canola). Foods that are naturally fattier, like meatballs, needn't be tossed in any additional oil. For foods that have been battered or dredged in flour, we recommend spraying the air fryer basket or rack first with cooking spray, laying your battered or dredged food in the basket or rack in a single layer, and then giving the food a light spritz of cooking spray just to coat the top. That little bit of oil is essential for getting foods to turn golden-brown, crisp, and appealing.

3. Fill the Air Fryer Basket or Rack

Battered and floured foods should be placed in one layer in an air fryer basket or rack. Some models offer racks that allow for two layers—if yours does, feel free to double up. For things like French fries or "roasted" vegetables, you can load the air fryer basket to the top; however, a fuller basket will require a longer cooking time and will result in food that's not quite as crisp as a basket with a smaller amount of food. It's also a good idea to give full baskets a shake every 3 to 5 minutes to make sure food is cooking evenly—many models will pause the timer when you open the drawer, expressly for this purpose.

4. Check for Doneness Early

Again, because the circulating air helps the air-fryer cooking environment maintain a more consistent temperature than other cooking methods, foods tend to cook faster in an air fryer than they do when being deep-fried or cooked in a conventional oven. That means if you're converting a recipe you already know and love to one cooked in an air fryer, you'll want to check the food about two-thirds of the way through the suggested cooking time to test doneness. Those fish sticks say they'll be done in 15 minutes? Check them at 10 minutes.

5. Make French Fries as Often as Possible

We know why you're really thinking about buying that air fryer, so here it is: yup, frozen French fries can be put right into the air fryer, no oil necessary, and cooked at 350°F for about 15 minutes. Be sure to give them a shake or a toss once or twice during cooking. Fresh-cut fries should first be soaked in hot water for at least 10 minutes (30 minutes is better) to remove excess starch. After soaking, drain and dry fries with a kitchen towel, toss in 1 to 2 tablespoons vegetable oil, then air fry at 350°F for about 20 minutes, again shaking once or twice during cooking. And in either case, don't forget to salt them when they're finished cooking.

How to Clean and Care for NuWave Air Fryer?

Traditionally, deep frying food is very messy. You end up with a lot of dirty pans, grimy utensils, and a greasy coating on everything around the fryer. Air fryers, on the other hand, are relatively clean. The cooking basket is completely enclosed, which eliminates splattering and all the fat, grease, and oil in your food drips down into the oil pan below. This doesn't mean there's no need to clean, however. Your air fryer should be cleaned every time you use it.

> ### To clean your NuWave air fryer:

✧ Unplug the air fryer from the wall socket and let it cool down.

✧ Wipe the outside with a damp cloth.

✧ Wash the pan, tray, and basket with hot water and dishwashing soap. All the air fryer's removable components are dishwasher safe, so they can be placed in a dishwasher if you would prefer not to wash them by hand.

✧ Clean in the inside of the air fryer with hot water and a cloth or sponge.

✧ If there is any food stuck to the heating element above the food basket, clean it off with a brush.

✧ Make sure the pan, tray, and basket are completely dry before putting them back into the air fryer.

> ### To care your NuWave air fryer:

Beyond regularly cleanings, your air fryer requires some basic maintenance to make sure that it doesn't get damaged or start functioning incorrectly. This includes:

✧ Inspecting the cords before each use. Never plug a damaged or frayed cord into an outlet. It can cause serious injury or even death. Make sure the cords are clean and damage-free before using your air fryer.

✧ Making sure the unit is clean and free of any debris before you start cooking. If it has been a long time since you last used your air fryer, check inside. Some dust may have accumulated. If there is any food residue on the basket for pan, clean it out before you start cooking.

✧ Make sure the air fryer is placed upright, on a level surface, before you start cooking.

✧ Make sure the air fryer is not placed close to a wall or another appliance. Air fryers need at least 4 inches of space behind them and 4 inches of space above them in order to adequately vent steam and hot air while cooking. Placing them in an enclosed space may cause the fryer to overheat.

✧ Visually inspect each component, including the basket, pan and handle prior to each use. If you find any damaged components, contact the manufacturer and get them replaced.

POULTRY RECIPES

Chicken Tikka

Servings: 4
Cooking Time: 15 Minutes

Ingredients:

- ¼ cup plain Greek yogurt
- 1 clove garlic, minced
- 1 tablespoon ketchup
- 1 tablespoon extra-virgin olive oil
- 1 tablespoon lemon juice
- ½ teaspoon salt
- ½ teaspoon ground cumin
- ½ teaspoon paprika
- ¼ teaspoon ground cinnamon
- ½ teaspoon ground black pepper
- ½ teaspoon cayenne pepper
- 1 pound boneless, skinless chicken thighs

Directions:

1. In a large bowl, stir together the yogurt, garlic, ketchup, olive oil, lemon juice, salt, cumin, paprika, cinnamon, black pepper, and cayenne pepper until combined.

2. Add the chicken thighs to the bow and fold the yogurt-spice mixture over the chicken thighs until they're covered with the marinade. Cover with plastic wrap and place in the refrigerator for 30 minutes.

3. When ready to cook the chicken, remove from the refrigerator and preheat the air fryer to 370°F.

4. Liberally spray the air fryer basket with olive oil mist. Place the chicken thighs into the air fryer basket, leaving space between the thighs to turn.

5. Cook for 10 minutes, turn the chicken thighs, and cook another 5 minutes (or until the internal temperature reaches 165°F).

6. Remove the chicken from the air fryer and serve warm with desired sides.

Tortilla Crusted Chicken Breast

Servings: 2
Cooking Time: 12 Minutes

Ingredients:

- ⅓ cup flour
- 1 teaspoon salt
- 1½ teaspoons chili powder
- 1 teaspoon ground cumin
- freshly ground black pepper
- 1 egg, beaten
- ¾ cup coarsely crushed yellow corn tortilla chips
- 2 (3- to 4-ounce) boneless chicken breasts
- vegetable oil
- ½ cup salsa
- ½ cup crumbled queso fresco
- fresh cilantro leaves
- sour cream or guacamole (optional)

Directions:

1. Set up a dredging station with three shallow dishes. Combine the flour, salt, chili powder, cumin and black pepper in the first shallow dish. Beat the egg in the second shallow dish. Place the crushed tortilla chips in the third shallow dish.

2. Dredge the chicken in the spiced flour, covering all sides of the breast. Then dip the chicken into the egg, coating the chicken completely. Finally, place the chicken into the tortilla chips and press the chips onto the chicken

to make sure they adhere to all sides of the breast. Spray the coated chicken breasts on both sides with vegetable oil.

3. Preheat the air fryer to 380°F.

4. Air-fry the chicken for 6 minutes. Then turn the chicken breasts over and air-fry for another 6 minutes. (Increase the cooking time if you are using chicken breasts larger than 3 to 4 ounces.)

5. When the chicken has finished cooking, serve each breast with a little salsa, the crumbled queso fresco and cilantro as the finishing touch. Serve some sour cream and/or guacamole at the table, if desired.

Chicken Cordon Bleu

Servings: 2
Cooking Time: 16 Minutes

Ingredients:

- 2 boneless, skinless chicken breasts
- ¼ teaspoon salt
- 2 teaspoons Dijon mustard
- 2 ounces deli ham
- 2 ounces Swiss, fontina, or Gruyère cheese
- ⅓ cup all-purpose flour
- 1 egg
- ½ cup breadcrumbs

Directions:

1. Pat the chicken breasts with a paper towel. Season the chicken with the salt. Pound the chicken breasts to 1½ inches thick. Create a pouch by slicing the side of each chicken breast. Spread 1 teaspoon Dijon mustard inside the pouch of each chicken breast. Wrap a 1-ounce slice of ham around a 1-ounce slice of cheese and place into the pouch. Repeat with the remaining ham and cheese.

2. In a medium bowl, place the flour.

3. In a second bowl, whisk the egg.

4. In a third bowl, place the breadcrumbs.

5. Dredge the chicken in the flour and shake off the excess. Next, dip the chicken into the egg and then in the breadcrumbs. Set the chicken on a plate and repeat with the remaining chicken piece.

6. Preheat the air fryer to 360°F.

7. Place the chicken in the air fryer basket and spray liberally with cooking spray. Cook for 8 minutes, turn the chicken breasts over, and liberally spray with cooking spray again; cook another 6 minutes. Once golden brown, check for an internal temperature of 165°F.

Southern-fried Chicken Livers

Servings: 4
Cooking Time: 12 Minutes

Ingredients:

- 2 eggs
- 2 tablespoons water
- ¾ cup flour
- 1½ cups panko breadcrumbs
- ½ cup plain breadcrumbs
- 1 teaspoon salt
- ½ teaspoon black pepper
- 20 ounces chicken livers, salted to taste
- oil for misting or cooking spray

Directions:

1. Beat together eggs and water in a shallow dish. Place the flour in a separate shallow dish.

2. In the bowl of a food processor, combine the panko, plain breadcrumbs, salt, and pepper. Process until well mixed and panko crumbs are finely crushed. Place crumbs in a third shallow dish.

3. Dip livers in flour, then egg wash, and then roll in panko mixture to coat well with crumbs.

4. Spray both sides of livers with oil or cooking spray. Cooking in two batches, place livers in air fryer basket in single layer.

5. Cook at 390°F for 7minutes. Spray livers, turn over, and spray again. Cook for 5 more minutes, until done inside and coating is golden brown.

6. Repeat to cook remaining livers.

Nacho Chicken Fries

Servings: 4

Cooking Time: 7 Minutes

Ingredients:

- 1 pound chicken tenders
- salt
- ¼ cup flour
- 2 eggs
- ¾ cup panko breadcrumbs
- ¾ cup crushed organic nacho cheese tortilla chips
- oil for misting or cooking spray
- Seasoning Mix
- 1 tablespoon chili powder
- 1 teaspoon ground cumin
- ½ teaspoon garlic powder
- ½ teaspoon onion powder

Directions:

1. Stir together all seasonings in a small cup and set aside.

2. Cut chicken tenders in half crosswise, then cut into strips no wider than about ½ inch.

3. Preheat air fryer to 390°F.

4. Salt chicken to taste. Place strips in large bowl and sprinkle with 1 tablespoon of the seasoning mix. Stir well to distribute seasonings.

5. Add flour to chicken and stir well to coat all sides.

6. Beat eggs together in a shallow dish.

7. In a second shallow dish, combine the panko, crushed chips, and the remaining 2 teaspoons of seasoning mix.

8. Dip chicken strips in eggs, then roll in crumbs. Mist with oil or cooking spray.

9. Chicken strips will cook best if done in two batches. They can be crowded and overlapping a little but not stacked in double or triple layers.

10. Cook for 4minutes. Shake basket, mist with oil, and cook 3 moreminutes, until chicken juices run clear and outside is crispy.

11. Repeat step 10 to cook remaining chicken fries.

Thai Turkey And Zucchini Meatballs

Servings: 4

Cooking Time: 12 Minutes

Ingredients:

- 1½ cups grated zucchini,
- squeezed dry in a clean kitchen towel (about 1 large zucchini)
- 3 scallions, finely chopped
- 2 cloves garlic, minced
- 1 tablespoon grated fresh ginger
- 1 tablespoon finely chopped fresh cilantro
- zest of 1 lime
- 1 teaspoon salt
- freshly ground black pepper
- 1½ pounds ground turkey (a mix of light and dark meat)
- 2 eggs, lightly beaten
- 1 cup Thai sweet chili sauce (spring roll sauce)
- lime wedges, for serving

Directions:

1. Combine the zucchini, scallions, garlic, ginger, cilantro, lime zest, salt, pepper, ground turkey

and eggs in a bowl and mix the ingredients together. Gently shape the mixture into 24 balls, about the size of golf balls.

2. Preheat the air fryer to 380°F.

3. Working in batches, air-fry the meatballs for 12 minutes, turning the meatballs over halfway through the cooking time. As soon as the meatballs have finished cooking, toss them in a bowl with the Thai sweet chili sauce to coat.

4. Serve the meatballs over rice noodles or white rice with the remaining Thai sweet chili sauce and lime wedges to squeeze over the top.

Spinach And Feta Stuffed Chicken Breasts

Servings: 4

Cooking Time: 27 Minutes

Ingredients:

- 1 (10-ounce) package frozen spinach, thawed and drained well
- 1 cup feta cheese, crumbled
- ½ teaspoon freshly ground black pepper
- 4 boneless chicken breasts
- salt and freshly ground black pepper
- 1 tablespoon olive oil

Directions:

1. Prepare the filling. Squeeze out as much liquid as possible from the thawed spinach. Rough chop the spinach and transfer it to a mixing bowl with the feta cheese and the freshly ground black pepper.

2. Prepare the chicken breast. Place the chicken breast on a cutting board and press down on the chicken breast with one hand to keep it stabilized. Make an incision about 1-inch long in the fattest side of the breast. Move the knife up and down inside the chicken breast, without poking through either the top or the bottom, or the other side of the breast. The inside pocket should be about 3-inches long, but the opening should only be about 1-inch wide. If this is too difficult, you can make the incision longer, but you will have to be more careful when cooking the chicken breast since this will expose more of the stuffing.

3. Once you have prepared the chicken breasts, use your fingers to stuff the filling into each pocket, spreading the mixture down as far as you can.

4. Preheat the air fryer to 380°F.

5. Lightly brush or spray the air fryer basket and the chicken breasts with olive oil. Transfer two of the stuffed chicken breasts to the air fryer. Air-fry for 12 minutes, turning the chicken breasts over halfway through the cooking time. Remove the chicken to a resting plate and air-fry the second two breasts for 12 minutes. Return the first batch of chicken to the air fryer with the second batch and air-fry for 3 more minutes. When the chicken is cooked, an instant read thermometer should register 165°F in the thickest part of the chicken, as well as in the stuffing.

6. Remove the chicken breasts and let them rest on a cutting board for 2 to 3 minutes. Slice the chicken on the bias and serve with the slices fanned out.

Parmesan Chicken Fingers

Servings: 2
Cooking Time: 19 Minutes

Ingredients:

- ½ cup flour
- 1 teaspoon salt
- freshly ground black pepper
- 2 eggs, beaten
- ¾ cup seasoned panko breadcrumbs
- ¾ cup grated Parmesan cheese
- 8 chicken tenders (about 1 pound)
- OR
- 2 to 3 boneless, skinless chicken breasts, cut into strips
- vegetable oil
- marinara sauce

Directions:

1. Set up a dredging station. Combine the flour, salt and pepper in a shallow dish. Place the beaten eggs in second shallow dish, and combine the panko breadcrumbs and Parmesan cheese in a third shallow dish.
2. Dredge the chicken tenders in the flour mixture. Then dip them into the egg, and finally place the chicken in the breadcrumb mixture. Press the coating onto both sides of the chicken tenders. Place the coated chicken tenders on a baking sheet until they are all coated. Spray both sides of the chicken fingers with vegetable oil.
3. Preheat the air fryer to 360°F.
4. Air-fry the chicken fingers in two batches. Transfer half the chicken fingers to the air fryer basket and air-fry for 9 minutes, turning the chicken over halfway through the cooking time. When the second batch of chicken fingers has finished cooking, return the first batch to the air fryer with the second batch and air-fry for one minute to heat everything through.
5. Serve immediately with marinara sauce, honey-mustard, ketchup or your favorite dipping sauce.

Maple Bacon Wrapped Chicken Breasts

Servings: 2
Cooking Time: 18 Minutes

Ingredients:

- 2 (6-ounce) boneless, skinless chicken breasts
- 2 tablespoons maple syrup, divided
- freshly ground black pepper
- 6 slices thick-sliced bacon
- fresh celery or parsley leaves
- Ranch Dressing:
- ¼ cup mayonnaise
- ¼ cup buttermilk
- ¼ cup Greek yogurt
- 1 tablespoon chopped fresh chives
- 1 tablespoon chopped fresh parsley
- 1 tablespoon chopped fresh dill
- 1 tablespoon lemon juice
- salt and freshly ground black pepper

Directions:

1. Brush the chicken breasts with half the maple syrup and season with freshly ground black pepper. Wrap three slices of bacon around each chicken breast, securing the ends with toothpicks.
2. Preheat the air fryer to 380°F.
3. Air-fry the chicken for 6 minutes. Then turn the chicken breasts over, pour more maple syrup on top and air-fry for another 6 minutes. Turn the chicken breasts one more time, brush the remaining maple syrup all over and continue to air-fry for a final 6 minutes.

4. While the chicken is cooking, prepare the dressing by combining all the dressing ingredients together in a bowl.

5. When the chicken has finished cooking, remove the toothpicks and serve each breast with a little dressing drizzled over each one. Scatter lots of fresh celery or parsley leaves on top.

Chicken Strips

Servings: 4
Cooking Time: 8 Minutes

Ingredients:
- 1 pound chicken tenders
- Marinade
- ¼ cup olive oil
- 2 tablespoons water
- 2 tablespoons honey
- 2 tablespoons white vinegar
- ½ teaspoon salt
- ½ teaspoon crushed red pepper
- 1 teaspoon garlic powder
- 1 teaspoon onion powder
- ½ teaspoon paprika

Directions:
1. Combine all marinade ingredients and mix well.
2. Add chicken and stir to coat. Cover tightly and let marinate in refrigerator for 30minutes.
3. Remove tenders from marinade and place them in a single layer in the air fryer basket.
4. Cook at 390°F for 3minutes. Turn tenders over and cook for 5 minutes longer or until chicken is done and juices run clear.
5. Repeat step 4 to cook remaining tenders.

Gluten-free Nutty Chicken Fingers

Servings: 4

Cooking Time: 10 Minutes

Ingredients:
- ½ cup gluten-free flour
- ½ teaspoon garlic powder
- ¼ teaspoon onion powder
- ¼ teaspoon black pepper
- ¼ teaspoon salt
- 1 cup walnuts, pulsed into coarse flour
- ½ cup gluten-free breadcrumbs
- 2 large eggs
- 1 pound boneless, skinless chicken tenders

Directions:
1. Preheat the air fryer to 400°F.
2. In a medium bowl, mix the flour, garlic, onion, pepper, and salt. Set aside.
3. In a separate bowl, mix the walnut flour and breadcrumbs.
4. In a third bowl, whisk the eggs.
5. Liberally spray the air fryer basket with olive oil spray.
6. Pat the chicken tenders dry with a paper towel. Dredge the tenders one at a time in the flour, then dip them in the egg, and toss them in the breadcrumb coating. Repeat until all tenders are coated.
7. Set each tender in the air fryer, leaving room on each side of the tender to allow for flipping.
8. When the basket is full, cook 5 minutes, flip, and cook another 5 minutes. Check the internal temperature after cooking completes; it should read 165°F. If it does not, cook another 2 to 4 minutes.
9. Remove the tenders and let cool 5 minutes before serving. Repeat until all the tenders are cooked.

Air-fried Turkey Breast With Cherry Glaze

Servings: 6

Cooking Time: 54 Minutes

Ingredients:

- 1 (5-pound) turkey breast
- 2 teaspoons olive oil
- 1 teaspoon dried thyme
- ½ teaspoon dried sage
- 1 teaspoon salt
- ½ teaspoon freshly ground black pepper
- ½ cup cherry preserves
- 1 tablespoon chopped fresh thyme leaves
- 1 teaspoon soy sauce*
- freshly ground black pepper

Directions:

1. All turkeys are built differently, so depending on the turkey breast and how your butcher has prepared it, you may need to trim the bottom of the ribs in order to get the turkey to sit upright in the air fryer basket without touching the heating element. The key to this recipe is getting the right size turkey breast. Once you've managed that, the rest is easy, so make sure your turkey breast fits into the air fryer basket before you Preheat the air fryer.

2. Preheat the air fryer to 350°F.

3. Brush the turkey breast all over with the olive oil. Combine the thyme, sage, salt and pepper and rub the outside of the turkey breast with the spice mixture.

4. Transfer the seasoned turkey breast to the air fryer basket, breast side up, and air-fry at 350°F for 25 minutes. Turn the turkey breast on its side and air-fry for another 12 minutes. Turn the turkey breast on the opposite side and air-fry for 12 more minutes. The internal temperature of the turkey breast should reach 165°F when fully cooked.

5. While the turkey is air-frying, make the glaze by combining the cherry preserves, fresh thyme, soy sauce and pepper in a small bowl. When the cooking time is up, return the turkey breast to an upright position and brush the glaze all over the turkey. Air-fry for a final 5 minutes, until the skin is nicely browned and crispy. Let the turkey rest, loosely tented with foil, for at least 5 minutes before slicing and serving.

Chicken Wellington

Servings: 2

Cooking Time: 31 Minutes

Ingredients:

- 2 (5-ounce) boneless, skinless chicken breasts
- ½ cup White Worcestershire sauce
- 3 tablespoons butter
- ½ cup finely diced onion (about ½ onion)
- 8 ounces button mushrooms, finely chopped
- ¼ cup chicken stock
- 2 tablespoons White Worcestershire sauce (or white wine)
- salt and freshly ground black pepper
- 1 tablespoon chopped fresh tarragon
- 2 sheets puff pastry, thawed
- 1 egg, beaten
- vegetable oil

Directions:

1. Place the chicken breasts in a shallow dish. Pour the White Worcestershire sauce over the chicken coating both sides and marinate for 30 minutes.

2. While the chicken is marinating, melt the butter in a large skillet over medium-high heat on

the stovetop. Add the onion and sauté for a few minutes, until it starts to soften. Add the mushrooms and sauté for 5 minutes until the vegetables are brown and soft. Deglaze the skillet with the chicken stock, scraping up any bits from the bottom of the pan. Add the White Worcestershire sauce and simmer for 3 minutes until the mixture reduces and starts to thicken. Season with salt and freshly ground black pepper. Remove the mushroom mixture from the heat and stir in the fresh tarragon. Let the mushroom mixture cool.

3. Preheat the air fryer to 360°F.

4. Remove the chicken from the marinade and transfer it to the air fryer basket. Tuck the small end of the chicken breast under the thicker part to shape it into a circle rather than an oval. Pour the marinade over the chicken and air-fry for 10 minutes.

5. Roll out the puff pastry and cut out two 6-inch squares. Brush the perimeter of each square with the egg wash. Place half of the mushroom mixture in the center of each puff pastry square. Place the chicken breasts, top side down on the mushroom mixture. Starting with one corner of puff pastry and working in one direction, pull the pastry up over the chicken to enclose it and press the ends of the pastry together in the middle. Brush the pastry with the egg wash to seal the edges. Turn the Wellingtons over and set aside.

6. To make a decorative design with the remaining puff pastry, cut out four 10-inch strips. For each Wellington, twist two of the strips together, place them over the chicken breast wrapped in puff pastry, and tuck the ends underneath to seal it. Brush the entire top and sides of the Wellingtons with the egg wash.

7. Preheat the air fryer to 350°F.

8. Spray or brush the air fryer basket with vegetable oil. Air-fry the chicken Wellingtons for 13 minutes. Carefully turn the Wellingtons over. Air-fry for another 8 minutes. Transfer to serving plates, light a candle and enjoy!

Mediterranean Stuffed Chicken Breasts

Servings: 4
Cooking Time: 24 Minutes

Ingredients:
- 4 boneless, skinless chicken breasts
- ½ teaspoon salt
- ½ teaspoon black pepper
- ½ teaspoon garlic powder
- ½ teaspoon paprika
- ½ cup canned artichoke hearts, chopped
- 4 ounces cream cheese
- ¼ cup grated Parmesan cheese

Directions:
1. Pat the chicken breasts with a paper towel. Using a sharp knife, cut a pouch in the side of each chicken breast for filling.

2. In a small bowl, mix the salt, pepper, garlic powder, and paprika. Season the chicken breasts with this mixture.

3. In a medium bowl, mix together the artichokes, cream cheese, and grated Parmesan cheese. Divide the filling between the 4 breasts, stuffing it inside the pouches. Use toothpicks to close the pouches and secure the filling.

4. Preheat the air fryer to 360°F.

5. Spray the air fryer basket liberally with cooking spray, add the stuffed chicken breasts to the basket, and spray liberally with cooking spray again. Cook for 14 minutes, carefully turn over

the chicken breasts, and cook another 10 minutes. Check the temperature at 20 minutes cooking. Chicken breasts are fully cooked when the center measures 165°F. Cook in batches, if needed.

Philly Chicken Cheesesteak Stromboli

Servings: 2
Cooking Time: 28 Minutes

Ingredients:
- ½ onion, sliced
- 1 teaspoon vegetable oil
- 2 boneless, skinless chicken breasts, partially frozen and sliced very thin on the bias (about 1 pound)
- 1 tablespoon Worcestershire sauce
- salt and freshly ground black pepper
- ½ recipe of Blue Jean Chef pizza dough (see page 229), or 14 ounces of store-bought pizza dough
- 1½ cups grated Cheddar cheese
- ½ cup Cheese Whiz® (or other jarred cheese sauce), warmed gently in the microwave
- tomato ketchup for serving

Directions:
1. Preheat the air fryer to 400°F.
2. Toss the sliced onion with oil and air-fry for 8 minutes, stirring halfway through the cooking time. Add the sliced chicken and Worcestershire sauce to the air fryer basket, and toss to evenly distribute the ingredients. Season the mixture with salt and freshly ground black pepper and air-fry for 8 minutes, stirring a couple of times during the cooking process. Remove the chicken and onion from the air fryer and let the mixture cool a little.

3. On a lightly floured surface, roll or press the pizza dough out into a 13-inch by 11-inch rectangle, with the long side closest to you. Sprinkle half of the Cheddar cheese over the dough leaving an empty 1-inch border from the edge farthest away from you. Top the cheese with the chicken and onion mixture, spreading it out evenly. Drizzle the cheese sauce over the meat and sprinkle the remaining Cheddar cheese on top.
4. Start rolling the stromboli away from you and toward the empty border. Make sure the filling stays tightly tucked inside the roll. Finally, tuck the ends of the dough in and pinch the seam shut. Place the seam side down and shape the Stromboli into a U-shape to fit in the air-fry basket. Cut 4 small slits with the tip of a sharp knife evenly in the top of the dough and lightly brush the stromboli with a little oil.
5. Preheat the air fryer to 370°F.
6. Spray or brush the air fryer basket with oil and transfer the U-shaped stromboli to the air fryer basket. Air-fry for 12 minutes, turning the stromboli over halfway through the cooking time. (Use a plate to invert the stromboli out of the air fryer basket and then slide it back into the basket off the plate.)
7. To remove, carefully flip stromboli over onto a cutting board. Let it rest for a couple of minutes before serving. Slice the stromboli into 3-inch pieces and serve with ketchup for dipping, if desired.

Italian Roasted Chicken Thighs

Servings: 6

Cooking Time: 14 Minutes

Ingredients:

- 6 boneless chicken thighs
- ½ teaspoon dried oregano
- ½ teaspoon garlic powder
- ½ teaspoon sea salt
- ½ teaspoon black pepper
- ¼ teaspoon crushed red pepper flakes

Directions:

1. Pat the chicken thighs with paper towel.
2. In a small bowl, mix the oregano, garlic powder, salt, pepper, and crushed red pepper flakes. Rub the spice mixture onto the chicken thighs.
3. Preheat the air fryer to 400°F.
4. Place the chicken thighs in the air fryer basket and spray with cooking spray. Cook for 10 minutes, turn over, and cook another 4 minutes. When cooking completes, the internal temperature should read 165°F.

Jerk Turkey Meatballs

Servings: 7

Cooking Time: 8 Minutes

Ingredients:

- 1 pound lean ground turkey
- ¼ cup chopped onion
- 1 teaspoon minced garlic
- ½ teaspoon dried thyme
- ¼ teaspoon ground cinnamon
- 1 teaspoon cayenne pepper
- ½ teaspoon paprika
- ½ teaspoon salt
- ⅛ teaspoon black pepper
- ¼ teaspoon red pepper flakes
- 2 teaspoons brown sugar
- 1 large egg, whisked
- ⅓ cup panko breadcrumbs
- 2⅓ cups cooked brown Jasmine rice
- 2 green onions, chopped
- ¾ cup sweet onion dressing

Directions:

1. Preheat the air fryer to 350°F.
2. In a medium bowl, mix the ground turkey with the onion, garlic, thyme, cinnamon, cayenne pepper, paprika, salt, pepper, red pepper flakes, and brown sugar. Add the whisked egg and stir in the breadcrumbs until the turkey starts to hold together.
3. Using a 1-ounce scoop, portion the turkey into meatballs. You should get about 28 meatballs.
4. Spray the air fryer basket with olive oil spray.
5. Place the meatballs into the air fryer basket and cook for 5 minutes, shake the basket, and cook another 2 to 4 minutes (or until the internal temperature of the meatballs reaches 165°F).
6. Remove the meatballs from the basket and repeat for the remaining meatballs.
7. Serve warm over a bed of rice with chopped green onions and spicy Caribbean jerk dressing.

Taquitos

Servings: 12

Cooking Time: 6 Minutes Per Batch

Ingredients:

- 1 teaspoon butter
- 2 tablespoons chopped green onions
- 1 cup cooked chicken, shredded
- 2 tablespoons chopped green chiles
- 2 ounces Pepper Jack cheese, shredded
- 4 tablespoons salsa

- ½ teaspoon lime juice
- ¼ teaspoon cumin
- ½ teaspoon chile powder
- ⅛ teaspoon garlic powder
- 12 corn tortillas
- oil for misting or cooking spray

Directions:

1. Melt butter in a saucepan over medium heat. Add green onions and sauté a minute or two, until tender.

2. Remove from heat and stir in the chicken, green chiles, cheese, salsa, lime juice, and seasonings.

3. Preheat air fryer to 390°F.

4. To soften refrigerated tortillas, wrap in damp paper towels and microwave for 30 to 60 seconds, until slightly warmed.

5. Remove one tortilla at a time, keeping others covered with the damp paper towels. Place a heaping tablespoon of filling into tortilla, roll up and secure with toothpick. Spray all sides with oil or cooking spray.

6. Place taquitos in air fryer basket, either in a single layer or stacked. To stack, leave plenty of space between taquitos and alternate the direction of the layers, 4 on the bottom lengthwise, then 4 more on top crosswise.

7. Cook for 6minutes or until brown and crispy.

8. Repeat steps 6 and 7 to cook remaining taquitos.

9. Serve hot with guacamole, sour cream, salsa or all three!

Buffalo Egg Rolls

Servings: 8
Cooking Time: 9 Minutes Per Batch

Ingredients:

- 1 teaspoon water
- 1 tablespoon cornstarch
- 1 egg
- 2½ cups cooked chicken, diced or shredded (see opposite page)
- ⅓ cup chopped green onion
- ⅓ cup diced celery
- ⅓ cup buffalo wing sauce
- 8 egg roll wraps
- oil for misting or cooking spray
- Blue Cheese Dip
- 3 ounces cream cheese, softened
- ⅓ cup blue cheese, crumbled
- 1 teaspoon Worcestershire sauce
- ¼ teaspoon garlic powder
- ¼ cup buttermilk (or sour cream)

Directions:

1. Mix water and cornstarch in a small bowl until dissolved. Add egg, beat well, and set aside.

2. In a medium size bowl, mix together chicken, green onion, celery, and buffalo wing sauce.

3. Divide chicken mixture evenly among 8 egg roll wraps, spooning ½ inch from one edge.

4. Moisten all edges of each wrap with beaten egg wash.

5. Fold the short ends over filling, then roll up tightly and press to seal edges.

6. Brush outside of wraps with egg wash, then spritz with oil or cooking spray.

7. Place 4 egg rolls in air fryer basket.

8. Cook at 390°F for 9minutes or until outside is brown and crispy.

9. While the rolls are cooking, prepare the Blue Cheese Dip. With a fork, mash together cream cheese and blue cheese.

10. Stir in remaining ingredients.

11. Dip should be just thick enough to slightly cling to egg rolls. If too thick, stir in buttermilk or milk 1 tablespoon at a time until you reach the desired consistency.

12. Cook remaining 4 egg rolls as in steps 7 and 8.

13. Serve while hot with Blue Cheese Dip, more buffalo wing sauce, or both.

Coconut Curry Chicken With Coconut Rice

Servings: 4
Cooking Time: 56 Minutes

Ingredients:

- 1 (14-ounce) can coconut milk
- 2 tablespoons green or red curry paste
- zest and juice of one lime
- 1 clove garlic, minced
- 1 tablespoon grated fresh ginger
- 1 teaspoon ground cumin
- 1 (3- to 4-pound) chicken, cut into 8 pieces
- vegetable or olive oil
- salt and freshly ground black pepper
- fresh cilantro leaves
- For the rice:
- 1 cup basmati or jasmine rice
- 1 cup water
- 1 cup coconut milk
- ½ teaspoon salt
- freshly ground black pepper

Directions:

1. Make the marinade by combining the coconut milk, curry paste, lime zest and juice, garlic, ginger and cumin. Coat the chicken on all sides with the marinade and marinate the chicken for 1 hour to overnight in the refrigerator.

2. Preheat the air fryer to 380°F.

3. Brush the bottom of the air fryer basket with oil. Transfer the chicken thighs and drumsticks from the marinade to the air fryer basket, letting most of the marinade drip off. Season to taste with salt and freshly ground black pepper.

4. Air-fry the chicken drumsticks and thighs at 380°F for 12 minutes. Flip the chicken over and continue to air-fry for another 12 minutes. Set aside and air-fry the chicken breast pieces at 380°F for 15 minutes. Turn the chicken breast pieces over and air-fry for another 12 minutes. Return the chicken thighs and drumsticks to the air fryer and air-fry for an additional 5 minutes.

5. While the chicken is cooking, make the coconut rice. Rinse the rice kernels with water and drain well. Place the rice in a medium saucepan with a tight fitting lid, along with the water, coconut milk, salt and freshly ground black pepper. Bring the mixture to a boil and then cover, reduce the heat and let it cook gently for 20 minutes without lifting the lid. When the time is up, lift the lid, fluff with a fork and set aside.

6. Remove the chicken from the air fryer and serve warm with the coconut rice and fresh cilantro scattered around.

Pecan Turkey Cutlets

Servings: 4
Cooking Time: 12 Minutes

Ingredients:

- ¾ cup panko breadcrumbs
- ¼ teaspoon salt
- ¼ teaspoon pepper
- ¼ teaspoon dry mustard
- ¼ teaspoon poultry seasoning
- ½ cup pecans
- ¼ cup cornstarch

- 1 egg, beaten
- 1 pound turkey cutlets, ½-inch thick
- salt and pepper
- oil for misting or cooking spray

Directions:

1. Place the panko crumbs, ¼ teaspoon salt, ¼ teaspoon pepper, mustard, and poultry seasoning in food processor. Process until crumbs are finely crushed. Add pecans and process in short pulses just until nuts are finely chopped. Go easy so you don't overdo it!

2. Preheat air fryer to 360°F.

3. Place cornstarch in one shallow dish and beaten egg in another. Transfer coating mixture from food processor into a third shallow dish.

4. Sprinkle turkey cutlets with salt and pepper to taste.

5. Dip cutlets in cornstarch and shake off excess. Then dip in beaten egg and roll in crumbs, pressing to coat well. Spray both sides with oil or cooking spray.

6. Place 2 cutlets in air fryer basket in a single layer and cook for 12 minutes or until juices run clear.

7. Repeat step 6 to cook remaining cutlets.

Tandoori Chicken Legs

Servings: 2
Cooking Time: 30 Minutes

Ingredients:

- 1 cup plain yogurt
- 2 cloves garlic, minced
- 1 tablespoon grated fresh ginger
- 2 teaspoons paprika
- 2 teaspoons ground coriander
- 1 teaspoon ground turmeric
- 1 teaspoon salt
- ¼ teaspoon ground cayenne pepper
- juice of 1 lime
- 2 bone-in, skin-on chicken legs
- fresh cilantro leaves

Directions:

1. Make the marinade by combining the yogurt, garlic, ginger, spices and lime juice. Make slashes into the chicken legs to help the marinade penetrate the meat. Pour the marinade over the chicken legs, cover and let the chicken marinate for at least an hour or overnight in the refrigerator.

2. Preheat the air fryer to 380°F.

3. Transfer the chicken legs from the marinade to the air fryer basket, reserving any extra marinade. Air-fry for 15 minutes. Flip the chicken over and pour the remaining marinade over the top. Air-fry for another 15 minutes, watching to make sure it doesn't brown too much. If it does start to get too brown, you can loosely tent the chicken with aluminum foil, tucking the ends of the foil under the chicken to stop it from blowing around.

4. Serve over rice with some fresh cilantro on top.

Spicy Black Bean Turkey Burgers With Cumin-avocado Spread

Servings: 2
Cooking Time: 20 Minutes

Ingredients:

- 1 cup canned black beans, drained and rinsed
- ¾ pound lean ground turkey
- 2 tablespoons minced red onion
- 1 Jalapeño pepper, seeded and minced
- 2 tablespoons plain breadcrumbs
- ½ teaspoon chili powder
- ¼ teaspoon cayenne pepper

- salt, to taste
- olive or vegetable oil
- 2 slices pepper jack cheese
- toasted burger rolls, sliced tomatoes, lettuce leaves
- Cumin-Avocado Spread:
- 1 ripe avocado
- juice of 1 lime
- 1 teaspoon ground cumin
- ½ teaspoon salt
- 1 tablespoon chopped fresh cilantro
- freshly ground black pepper

Directions:

1. Place the black beans in a large bowl and smash them slightly with the back of a fork. Add the ground turkey, red onion, Jalapeño pepper, breadcrumbs, chili powder and cayenne pepper. Season with salt. Mix with your hands to combine all the ingredients and then shape them into 2 patties. Brush both sides of the burger patties with a little olive or vegetable oil.

2. Preheat the air fryer to 380°F.

3. Transfer the burgers to the air fryer basket and air-fry for 20 minutes, flipping them over halfway through the cooking process. Top the burgers with the pepper jack cheese (securing the slices to the burgers with a toothpick) for the last 2 minutes of the cooking process.

4. While the burgers are cooking, make the cumin avocado spread. Place the avocado, lime juice, cumin and salt in food processor and process until smooth. (For a chunkier spread, you can mash this by hand in a bowl.) Stir in the cilantro and season with freshly ground black pepper. Chill the spread until you are ready to serve.

5. When the burgers have finished cooking, remove them from the air fryer and let them rest on a plate, covered gently with aluminum foil. Brush a little olive oil on the insides of the burger rolls. Place the rolls, cut side up, into the air fryer basket and air-fry at 400°F for 1 minute to toast and warm them.

6. Spread the cumin-avocado spread on the rolls and build your burgers with lettuce and sliced tomatoes and any other ingredient you like. Serve warm with a side of sweet potato fries.

Buttermilk-fried Drumsticks

Servings: 2
Cooking Time: 25 Minutes

Ingredients:

- 1 egg
- ½ cup buttermilk
- ¾ cup self-rising flour
- ¾ cup seasoned panko breadcrumbs
- 1 teaspoon salt
- ¼ teaspoon ground black pepper (to mix into coating)
- 4 chicken drumsticks, skin on
- oil for misting or cooking spray

Directions:

1. Beat together egg and buttermilk in shallow dish.

2. In a second shallow dish, combine the flour, panko crumbs, salt, and pepper.

3. Sprinkle chicken legs with additional salt and pepper to taste.

4. Dip legs in buttermilk mixture, then roll in panko mixture, pressing in crumbs to make coating stick. Mist with oil or cooking spray.

5. Spray air fryer basket with cooking spray.

6. Cook drumsticks at 360°F for 10minutes. Turn pieces over and cook an additional 10minutes.

7. Turn pieces to check for browning. If you have any white spots that haven't begun to brown, spritz them with oil or cooking spray. Continue cooking for 5 more minutes or until crust is golden brown and juices run clear. Larger, meatier drumsticks will take longer to cook than small ones.

Chicken Fried Steak With Gravy

Servings: 4

Cooking Time: 10 Minutes Per Batch

Ingredients:

- ½ cup flour
- 2 teaspoons salt, divided
- freshly ground black pepper
- ¼ teaspoon garlic powder
- 1 cup buttermilk
- 1 cup fine breadcrumbs
- 4 tenderized top round steaks (about 6 to 8 ounces each; ½-inch thick)
- vegetable or canola oil
- For the Gravy:
- 2 tablespoons butter or bacon drippings
- ¼ onion, minced (about ¼ cup)
- 1 clove garlic, smashed
- ¼ teaspoon dried thyme
- 3 tablespoons flour
- 1 cup milk
- salt and lots of freshly ground black pepper
- a few dashes of Worcestershire sauce

Directions:

1. Set up a dredging station. Combine the flour, 1 teaspoon of salt, black pepper and garlic powder in a shallow bowl. Pour the buttermilk into a second shallow bowl. Finally, put the breadcrumbs and 1 teaspoon of salt in a third shallow bowl.

2. Dip the tenderized steaks into the flour, then the buttermilk, and then the breadcrumb mixture, pressing the crumbs onto the steak. Place them on a baking sheet and spray both sides generously with vegetable or canola oil.

3. Preheat the air fryer to 400°F.

4. Transfer the steaks to the air fryer basket, two at a time, and air-fry for 10 minutes, flipping the steaks over halfway through the cooking time. This will cook your steaks to medium. If you want the steaks cooked a little more or less, add or subtract a minute or two. Hold the first batch of steaks warm in a 170°F oven while you cook the second batch.

5. While the steaks are cooking, make the gravy. Melt the butter in a small saucepan over medium heat on the stovetop. Add the onion, garlic and thyme and cook for five minutes, until the onion is soft and just starting to brown. Stir in the flour and cook for another five minutes, stirring regularly, until the mixture starts to brown. Whisk in the milk and bring the mixture to a boil to thicken. Season to taste with salt, lots of freshly ground black pepper and a few dashes of Worcestershire sauce.

6. Plate the chicken fried steaks with mashed potatoes and vegetables and serve the gravy at the table to pour over the top.

BEEF , PORK & LAMB RECIPES

Pork Loin

Servings: 8
Cooking Time: 50 Minutes

Ingredients:

- 1 tablespoon lime juice
- 1 tablespoon orange marmalade
- 1 teaspoon coarse brown mustard
- 1 teaspoon curry powder
- 1 teaspoon dried lemongrass
- 2-pound boneless pork loin roast
- salt and pepper
- cooking spray

Directions:

1. Mix together the lime juice, marmalade, mustard, curry powder, and lemongrass.
2. Rub mixture all over the surface of the pork loin. Season to taste with salt and pepper.
3. Spray air fryer basket with nonstick spray and place pork roast diagonally in basket.
4. Cook at 360°F for approximately 50 minutes, until roast registers 130°F on a meat thermometer.
5. Wrap roast in foil and let rest for 10minutes before slicing.

Tuscan Veal Chops

Servings: 2
Cooking Time: 12-15 Minutes

Ingredients:

- 4 teaspoons Olive oil
- 2 teaspoons Finely minced garlic
- 2 teaspoons Finely minced fresh rosemary leaves
- 1 teaspoon Finely grated lemon zest
- 1 teaspoon Crushed fennel seeds
- 1 teaspoon Table salt
- Up to ¼ teaspoon Red pepper flakes
- 2 10-ounce bone-in veal loin or rib chop(s), about ½ inch thick

Directions:

1. Preheat the air fryer to 400°F.
2. Mix the oil, garlic, rosemary, lemon zest, fennel seeds, salt, and red pepper flakes in a small bowl. Rub this mixture onto both sides of the veal chop(s). Set aside at room temperature as the machine comes to temperature.
3. Set the chop(s) in the basket. If you're cooking more than one chop, leave as much air space between them as possible. Air-fry undisturbed for 12 minutes for medium-rare, or until an instant-read meat thermometer inserted into the center of a chop (without touching bone) registers 135°F (not USDA-approved). Or air-fry undisturbed for 15 minutes for medium-well, or until an instant-read meat thermometer registers 145°F (USDA-approved).
4. Use kitchen tongs to transfer the chops to a cutting board or a wire rack. Cool for 5 minutes before serving.

Beef Al Carbon (street Taco Meat)

Servings: 6
Cooking Time: 8 Minutes

Ingredients:

- 1½ pounds sirloin steak, cut into ½-inch cubes
- ¾ cup lime juice
- ½ cup extra-virgin olive oil
- 1 teaspoon ground cumin

- 2 teaspoons garlic powder
- 1 teaspoon salt

Directions:

1. In a large bowl, toss together the steak, lime juice, olive oil, cumin, garlic powder, and salt. Allow the meat to marinate for 30 minutes. Drain off all the marinade and pat the meat dry with paper towels.

2. Preheat the air fryer to 400°F.

3. Place the meat in the air fryer basket and spray with cooking spray. Cook the meat for 5 minutes, toss the meat, and continue cooking another 3 minutes, until slightly crispy.

Flank Steak With Roasted Peppers And Chimichurri

Servings: 4
Cooking Time: 22 Minutes

Ingredients:

- 2 cups flat-leaf parsley leaves
- ¼ cup fresh oregano leaves
- 3 cloves garlic
- ½ cup olive oil
- ¼ cup red wine vinegar
- ½ teaspoon salt
- freshly ground black pepper
- ¼ teaspoon crushed red pepper flakes
- ½ teaspoon ground cumin
- 1 pound flank steak
- 1 red bell pepper, cut into strips
- 1 yellow bell pepper, cut into strips

Directions:

1. Make the chimichurri sauce by chopping the parsley, oregano and garlic in a food processor. Add the olive oil, vinegar and seasonings and process again. Pour half of the sauce into a shallow dish with the flank steak and set the remaining sauce aside. Pierce the flank steak with a needle-style meat tenderizer or a paring knife and marinate the steak for 2 to 24 hours in the refrigerator. When you are ready to cook, remove the steak from the refrigerator and let it sit at room temperature for 30 minutes.

2. Preheat the air fryer to 400°F.

3. Cut the flank steak in half so that it fits more easily into the air fryer and transfer both pieces to the air fryer basket. Air-fry for 14 minutes, depending on how you like your steak cooked (10 minutes will give you medium for a 1-inch thick flank steak). Flip the steak over halfway through the cooking time.

4. When the flank steak is cooked to your liking, transfer it to a cutting board, loosely tent with foil and let it rest while you cook the peppers.

5. Toss the peppers in a little olive oil, salt and freshly ground black pepper and transfer them to the air fryer basket. Air-fry at 400°F for 8 minutes, shaking the basket once or twice throughout the cooking process. To serve, slice the flank steak against the grain of the meat and top with the roasted peppers. Drizzle the reserved chimichurri sauce on top, thinning the sauce with another tablespoon of olive oil if desired.

Easy Tex-mex Chimichangas

Servings: 2
Cooking Time: 8 Minutes

Ingredients:

- ¼ pound Thinly sliced deli roast beef, chopped
- ½ cup (about 2 ounces) Shredded Cheddar cheese or shredded Tex-Mex cheese blend
- ¼ cup Jarred salsa verde or salsa rojo
- ½ teaspoon Ground cumin
- ½ teaspoon Dried oregano
- 2 Burrito-size (12-inch) flour tortilla(s), not corn tortillas (gluten-free, if a concern)
- ⅔ cup Canned refried beans
- Vegetable oil spray

Directions:

1. Preheat the air fryer to 375°F .
2. Stir the roast beef, cheese, salsa, cumin, and oregano in a bowl until well mixed.
3. Lay a tortilla on a clean, dry work surface. Spread ⅓ cup of the refried beans in the center lower third of the tortilla(s), leaving an inch on either side of the spread beans.
4. For one chimichanga, spread all of the roast beef mixture on top of the beans. For two, spread half of the roast beef mixture on each tortilla.
5. At either "end" of the filling mixture, fold the sides of the tortilla up and over the filling, partially covering it. Starting with the unfolded side of the tortilla just below the filling, roll the tortilla closed. Fold and roll the second filled tortilla, as necessary.
6. Coat the exterior of the tortilla(s) with vegetable oil spray. Set the chimichanga(s) seam side down in the basket, with at least ½ inch air space between them if you're working with two.

Air-fry undisturbed for 8 minutes, or until the tortilla is lightly browned and crisp.

7. Use kitchen tongs to gently transfer the chimichanga(s) to a wire rack. Cool for at last 5 minutes or up to 20 minutes before serving.

Vietnamese Shaking Beef

Servings: 3
Cooking Time: 7 Minutes

Ingredients:

- 1 pound Beef tenderloin, cut into 1-inch cubes
- 1 tablespoon Regular or low-sodium soy sauce or gluten-free tamari sauce
- 1 tablespoon Fish sauce (gluten-free, if a concern)
- 1 tablespoon Dark brown sugar
- 1½ teaspoons Ground black pepper
- 3 Medium scallions, trimmed and thinly sliced
- 2 tablespoons Butter
- 1½ teaspoons Minced garlic

Directions:

1. Mix the beef, soy or tamari sauce, fish sauce, and brown sugar in a bowl until well combined. Cover and refrigerate for at least 2 hours or up to 8 hours, tossing the beef at least twice in the marinade.
2. Put a 6-inch round or square cake pan in an air-fryer basket for a small batch, a 7-inch round or square cake pan for a medium batch, or an 8-inch round or square cake pan for a large one. Or put one of these on the rack of a toaster oven–style air fryer. Heat the machine with the pan in it to 400°F. When the machine it at temperature, let the pan sit in the heat for 2 to 3 minutes so that it gets very hot.

3. Use a slotted spoon to transfer the beef to the pan, leaving any marinade behind in the bowl. Spread the meat into as close to an even layer as you can. Air-fry undisturbed for 5 minutes. Meanwhile, discard the marinade, if any.

4. Add the scallions, butter, and garlic to the beef. Air-fry for 2 minutes, tossing and rearranging the beef and scallions repeatedly, perhaps every 20 seconds.

5. Remove the basket from the machine and let the meat cool in the pan for a couple of minutes before serving.

Meatball Subs

Servings: 4
Cooking Time: 11 Minutes

Ingredients:
- Marinara Sauce
- 1 15-ounce can diced tomatoes
- 1 teaspoon garlic powder
- 1 teaspoon dried basil
- ½ teaspoon oregano
- ⅛ teaspoon salt
- 1 tablespoon robust olive oil
- Meatballs
- ¼ pound ground turkey
- ¾ pound very lean ground beef
- 1 tablespoon milk
- ½ cup torn bread pieces
- 1 egg
- ¼ teaspoon salt
- ½ teaspoon dried onion
- 1 teaspoon garlic powder
- ¼ teaspoon smoked paprika
- ¼ teaspoon crushed red pepper
- 1½ teaspoons dried parsley
- ¼ teaspoon oregano
- 2 teaspoons Worcestershire sauce
- Sandwiches
- 4 large whole-grain sub or hoagie rolls, split
- toppings, sliced or chopped:
- mushrooms
- jalapeño or banana peppers
- red or green bell pepper
- red onions
- grated cheese

Directions:

1. Place all marinara ingredients in saucepan and bring to a boil. Lower heat and simmer 10minutes, uncovered.

2. Combine all meatball ingredients in large bowl and stir. Mixture should be well blended but don't overwork it. Excessive mixing will toughen the meatballs.

3. Divide meat into 16 equal portions and shape into balls.

4. Cook the balls at 360°F until meat is done and juices run clear, about 11 minutes.

5. While meatballs are cooking, taste marinara. If you prefer stronger flavors, add more seasoning and simmer another 5minutes.

6. When meatballs finish cooking, drain them on paper towels.

7. To assemble subs, place 4 meatballs on each sub roll, spoon sauce over meat, and add preferred toppings. Serve with additional marinara for dipping.

Brie And Cranberry Burgers

Servings: 3
Cooking Time: 9 Minutes

Ingredients:
- 1 pound ground beef (80% lean)
- 1 tablespoon chopped fresh thyme

- 1 tablespoon Worcestershire sauce
- ½ teaspoon salt
- freshly ground black pepper
- 1 (4-ounce) wheel of Brie cheese, sliced
- handful of arugula
- 3 or 4 brioche hamburger buns (or potato hamburger buns), toasted
- ¼ to ½ cup whole berry cranberry sauce

Directions:

1. Combine the beef, thyme, Worcestershire sauce, salt and pepper together in a large bowl and mix well. Divide the meat into 4 (¼-pound) portions or 3 larger portions and then form them into burger patties, being careful not to over-handle the meat.

2. Preheat the air fryer to 390°F and pour a little water into the bottom of the air fryer drawer. (This will help prevent the grease that drips into the bottom drawer from burning and smoking.)

3. Transfer the burgers to the air fryer basket. Air-fry the burgers at 390°F for 5 minutes. Flip the burgers over and air-fry for another 2 minutes. Top each burger with a couple slices of brie and air-fry for another minute or two, just to soften the cheese.

4. Build the burgers by placing a few leaves of arugula on the bottom bun, adding the burger and a spoonful of cranberry sauce on top. Top with the other half of the hamburger bun and enjoy.

Sweet And Sour Pork

Servings: 2
Cooking Time: 11 Minutes

Ingredients:

- ⅓ cup all-purpose flour
- ⅓ cup cornstarch
- 2 teaspoons Chinese 5-spice powder
- 1 teaspoon salt
- freshly ground black pepper
- 1 egg
- 2 tablespoons milk
- ¾ pound boneless pork, cut into 1-inch cubes
- vegetable or canola oil, in a spray bottle
- 1½ cups large chunks of red and green peppers
- ½ cup ketchup
- 2 tablespoons rice wine vinegar or apple cider vinegar
- 2 tablespoons brown sugar
- ¼ cup orange juice
- 1 tablespoon soy sauce
- 1 clove garlic, minced
- 1 cup cubed pineapple
- chopped scallions

Directions:

1. Set up a dredging station with two bowls. Combine the flour, cornstarch, Chinese 5-spice powder, salt and pepper in one large bowl. Whisk the egg and milk together in a second bowl. Dredge the pork cubes in the flour mixture first, then dip them into the egg and then back into the flour to coat on all sides. Spray the coated pork cubes with vegetable or canola oil.

2. Preheat the air fryer to 400°F.

3. Toss the pepper chunks with a little oil and air-fry at 400°F for 5 minutes, shaking the basket halfway through the cooking time.

4. While the peppers are cooking, start making the sauce. Combine the ketchup, rice wine vinegar, brown sugar, orange juice, soy sauce, and garlic in a medium saucepan and bring the mixture to a boil on the stovetop. Reduce the heat and simmer for 5 minutes. When the peppers

have finished air-frying, add them to the saucepan along with the pineapple chunks. Simmer the peppers and pineapple in the sauce for an additional 2 minutes. Set aside and keep warm.

5. Add the dredged pork cubes to the air fryer basket and air-fry at 400°F for 6 minutes, shaking the basket to turn the cubes over for the last minute of the cooking process.

6. When ready to serve, toss the cooked pork with the pineapple, peppers and sauce. Serve over white rice and garnish with chopped scallions.

Crispy Pork Medallions With Radicchio And Endive Salad

Servings: 4
Cooking Time: 7 Minutes

Ingredients:
- 1 (8-ounce) pork tenderloin
- salt and freshly ground black pepper
- ¼ cup flour
- 2 eggs, lightly beaten
- ¾ cup cracker meal
- 1 teaspoon paprika
- 1 teaspoon dry mustard
- 1 teaspoon garlic powder
- 1 teaspoon dried thyme
- 1 teaspoon salt
- vegetable or canola oil, in spray bottle
- Vinaigrette
- ¼ cup white balsamic vinegar
- 2 tablespoons agave syrup (or honey or maple syrup)
- 1 tablespoon Dijon mustard
- juice of ½ lemon
- 2 tablespoons chopped chervil or flat-leaf parsley
- salt and freshly ground black pepper
- ½ cup extra-virgin olive oil
- Radicchio and Endive Salad
- 1 heart romaine lettuce, torn into large pieces
- ½ head radicchio, coarsely chopped
- 2 heads endive, sliced
- ½ cup cherry tomatoes, halved
- 3 ounces fresh mozzarella, diced
- salt and freshly ground black pepper

Directions:
1. Slice the pork tenderloin into 1-inch slices. Using a meat pounder, pound the pork slices into thin ½-inch medallions. Generously season the pork with salt and freshly ground black pepper on both sides.

2. Set up a dredging station using three shallow dishes. Place the flour in one dish and the beaten eggs in a second dish. Combine the cracker meal, paprika, dry mustard, garlic powder, thyme and salt in a third dish.

3. Preheat the air fryer to 400°F.

4. Dredge the pork medallions in flour first and then into the beaten egg. Let the excess egg drip off and coat both sides of the medallions with the cracker meal crumb mixture. Spray both sides of the coated medallions with vegetable or canola oil.

5. Air-fry the medallions in two batches at 400°F for 5 minutes. Once you have air-fried all the medallions, flip them all over and return the first batch of medallions back into the air fryer on top of the second batch. Air-fry at 400°F for an additional 2 minutes.

6. While the medallions are cooking, make the salad and dressing. Whisk the white balsamic vinegar, agave syrup, Dijon mustard, lemon juice, chervil, salt and pepper together in a small bowl.

Whisk in the olive oil slowly until combined and thickened.

7. Combine the romaine lettuce, radicchio, endive, cherry tomatoes, and mozzarella cheese in a large salad bowl. Drizzle the dressing over the vegetables and toss to combine. Season with salt and freshly ground black pepper.

8. Serve the pork medallions warm on or beside the salad.

Barbecue-style London Broil

Servings: 5
Cooking Time: 17 Minutes

Ingredients:
- ¾ teaspoon Mild smoked paprika
- ¾ teaspoon Dried oregano
- ¾ teaspoon Table salt
- ¾ teaspoon Ground black pepper
- ¼ teaspoon Garlic powder
- ¼ teaspoon Onion powder
- 1½ pounds Beef London broil (in one piece)
- Olive oil spray

Directions:
1. Preheat the air fryer to 400°F.
2. Mix the smoked paprika, oregano, salt, pepper, garlic powder, and onion powder in a small bowl until uniform.
3. Pat and rub this mixture across all surfaces of the beef. Lightly coat the beef on all sides with olive oil spray.
4. When the machine is at temperature, lay the London broil flat in the basket and air-fry undisturbed for 8 minutes for the small batch, 10 minutes for the medium batch, or 12 minutes for the large batch for medium-rare, until an instant-read meat thermometer inserted into the center of the meat registers 130°F (not USDA-approved).

Add 1, 2, or 3 minutes, respectively (based on the size of the cut) for medium, until an instant-read meat thermometer registers 135°F (not USDA-approved). Or add 3, 4, or 5 minutes respectively for medium, until an instant-read meat thermometer registers 145°F (USDA-approved).

5. Use kitchen tongs to transfer the London broil to a cutting board. Let the meat rest for 10 minutes. It needs a long time for the juices to be reincorporated into the meat's fibers. Carve it against the grain into very thin (less than ¼-inch-thick) slices to serve.

City "chicken"

Servings: 3
Cooking Time: 10 Minutes

Ingredients:
- 1 pound Pork tenderloin, cut into 2-inch cubes
- ½ cup All-purpose flour or tapioca flour
- 1 Large egg(s)
- 1 teaspoon Dried poultry seasoning blend
- 1¼ cups Plain panko bread crumbs (gluten-free, if a concern)
- Vegetable oil spray

Directions:
1. Preheat the air fryer to 350°F .
2. Thread 3 or 4 pieces of pork on a 4-inch bamboo skewer. You'll need 2 or 3 skewers for a small batch, 3 or 4 for a medium, and up to 6 for a large batch.
3. Set up and fill three shallow soup plates or small pie plates on your counter: one for the flour; one for the egg(s), beaten with the poultry seasoning until foamy; and one for the bread crumbs.

4. Dip and roll one skewer into the flour, coating all sides of the meat. Gently shake off any excess flour, then dip and roll the skewer in the egg mixture. Let any excess egg mixture slip back into the rest, then set the skewer in the bread crumbs and roll it around, pressing gently, until the exterior surfaces of the meat are evenly coated. Generously coat the meat on the skewer with vegetable oil spray. Set aside and continue dredging, dipping, coating, and spraying the remaining skewers.

5. Set the skewers in the basket in one layer and air-fry undisturbed for 10 minutes, or until brown and crunchy.

6. Use kitchen tongs to transfer the skewers to a wire rack. Cool for a minute or two before serving.

Honey Mesquite Pork Chops

Servings: 2
Cooking Time: 10 Minutes

Ingredients:
- 2 tablespoons mesquite seasoning
- ¼ cup honey
- 1 tablespoon olive oil
- 1 tablespoon water
- freshly ground black pepper
- 2 bone-in center cut pork chops (about 1 pound)

Directions:
1. Whisk the mesquite seasoning, honey, olive oil, water and freshly ground black pepper together in a shallow glass dish. Pierce the chops all over and on both sides with a fork or meat tenderizer. Add the pork chops to the marinade and massage the marinade into the chops. Cover and marinate for 30 minutes.
2. Preheat the air fryer to 330°F.

3. Transfer the pork chops to the air fryer basket and pour half of the marinade over the chops, reserving the remaining marinade. Air-fry the pork chops for 6 minutes. Flip the pork chops over and pour the remaining marinade on top. Air-fry for an additional 3 minutes at 330°F. Then, increase the air fryer temperature to 400°F and air-fry the pork chops for an additional minute.

4. Transfer the pork chops to a serving plate, and let them rest for 5 minutes before serving. If you'd like a sauce for these chops, pour the cooked marinade from the bottom of the air fryer over the top.

Pork Cutlets With Almond-lemon Crust

Servings: 3
Cooking Time: 14 Minutes

Ingredients:
- ¾ cup Almond flour
- ¾ cup Plain dried bread crumbs (gluten-free, if a concern)
- 1½ teaspoons Finely grated lemon zest
- 1¼ teaspoons Table salt
- ¾ teaspoon Garlic powder
- ¾ teaspoon Dried oregano
- 1 Large egg white(s)
- 2 tablespoons Water
- 3 6-ounce center-cut boneless pork loin chops (about ¾ inch thick)
- Olive oil spray

Directions:
1. Preheat the air fryer to 375°F .
2. Mix the almond flour, bread crumbs, lemon zest, salt, garlic powder, and dried oregano in a large bowl until well combined.

3. Whisk the egg white(s) and water in a shallow soup plate or small pie plate until uniform.

4. Dip a chop in the egg white mixture, turning it to coat all sides, even the ends. Let any excess egg white mixture slip back into the rest, then set it in the almond flour mixture. Turn it several times, pressing gently to coat it evenly. Generously coat the chop with olive oil spray, then set aside to dip and coat the remaining chop(s).

5. Set the chops in the basket with as much air space between them as possible. Air-fry undisturbed for 12 minutes, or until browned and crunchy. You may need to add 2 minutes to the cooking time if the machine is at 360°F.

6. Use kitchen tongs to transfer the chops to a wire rack. Cool for a few minutes before serving.

Calf's Liver

Servings: 4
Cooking Time: 5 Minutes

Ingredients:

- 1 pound sliced calf's liver
- salt and pepper
- 2 eggs
- 2 tablespoons milk
- ½ cup whole wheat flour
- 1½ cups panko breadcrumbs
- ½ cup plain breadcrumbs
- ½ teaspoon salt
- ¼ teaspoon pepper
- oil for misting or cooking spray

Directions:

1. Cut liver slices crosswise into strips about ½-inch wide. Sprinkle with salt and pepper to taste.

2. Beat together egg and milk in a shallow dish.

3. Place wheat flour in a second shallow dish.

4. In a third shallow dish, mix together panko, plain breadcrumbs, ½ teaspoon salt, and ¼ teaspoon pepper.

5. Preheat air fryer to 390°F.

6. Dip liver strips in flour, egg wash, and then breadcrumbs, pressing in coating slightly to make crumbs stick.

7. Cooking half the liver at a time, place strips in air fryer basket in a single layer, close but not touching. Cook at 390°F for 5 minutes or until done to your preference.

8. Repeat step 7 to cook remaining liver.

Lamb Chops

Servings: 2
Cooking Time: 20 Minutes

Ingredients:

- 2 teaspoons oil
- ½ teaspoon ground rosemary
- ½ teaspoon lemon juice
- 1 pound lamb chops, approximately 1-inch thick
- salt and pepper
- cooking spray

Directions:

1. Mix the oil, rosemary, and lemon juice together and rub into all sides of the lamb chops. Season to taste with salt and pepper.

2. For best flavor, cover lamb chops and allow them to rest in the fridge for 20 minutes.

3. Spray air fryer basket with nonstick spray and place lamb chops in it.

4. Cook at 360°F for approximately 20minutes. This will cook chops to medium. The meat will be juicy but have no remaining pink. Cook for a minute or two longer for well done chops. For

rare chops, stop cooking after about 12minutes and check for doneness.

Pork Taco Gorditas

Servings: 4
Cooking Time: 21 Minutes

Ingredients:

- 1 pound lean ground pork
- 2 tablespoons chili powder
- 2 tablespoons ground cumin
- 1 teaspoon dried oregano
- 2 teaspoons paprika
- 1 teaspoon garlic powder
- ½ cup water
- 1 (15-ounce) can pinto beans, drained and rinsed
- ½ cup taco sauce
- salt and freshly ground black pepper
- 2 cups grated Cheddar cheese
- 5 (12-inch) flour tortillas
- 4 (8-inch) crispy corn tortilla shells
- 4 cups shredded lettuce
- 1 tomato, diced
- ⅓ cup sliced black olives
- sour cream, for serving
- tomato salsa, for serving

Directions:

1. Preheat the air fryer to 400°F.
2. Place the ground pork in the air fryer basket and air-fry at 400°F for 10 minutes, stirring a few times during the cooking process to gently break up the meat. Combine the chili powder, cumin, oregano, paprika, garlic powder and water in a small bowl. Stir the spice mixture into the browned pork. Stir in the beans and taco sauce and air-fry for an additional minute. Transfer the pork mixture to a bowl. Season to taste with salt and freshly ground black pepper.
3. Sprinkle ½ cup of the shredded cheese in the center of four of the flour tortillas, making sure to leave a 2-inch border around the edge free of cheese and filling. Divide the pork mixture among the four tortillas, placing it on top of the cheese. Place a crunchy corn tortilla on top of the pork and top with shredded lettuce, diced tomatoes, and black olives. Cut the remaining flour tortilla into 4 quarters. These quarters of tortilla will serve as the bottom of the gordita. Place one quarter tortilla on top of each gordita and fold the edges of the bottom flour tortilla up over the sides, enclosing the filling. While holding the seams down, brush the bottom of the gordita with olive oil and place the seam side down on the countertop while you finish the remaining three gorditas.
4. Preheat the air fryer to 380°F.
5. Air-fry one gordita at a time. Transfer the gordita carefully to the air fryer basket, seam side down. Brush or spray the top tortilla with oil and air-fry for 5 minutes. Carefully turn the gordita over and air-fry for an additional 5 minutes, until both sides are browned. When finished air frying all four gorditas, layer them back into the air fryer for an additional minute to make sure they are all warm before serving with sour cream and salsa.

Pork Schnitzel

Servings: 4

Cooking Time: 14 Minutes

Ingredients:

- 4 boneless pork chops, pounded to ¼-inch thickness
- 1 teaspoon salt, divided
- 1 teaspoon black pepper, divided
- ½ cup all-purpose flour
- 2 eggs
- 1 cup breadcrumbs
- ¼ teaspoon paprika
- 1 lemon, cut into wedges

Directions:

1. Season both sides of the pork chops with ½ teaspoon of the salt and ½ teaspoon of the pepper.
2. On a plate, place the flour.
3. In a large bowl, whisk the eggs.
4. In another large bowl, place the breadcrumbs.
5. Season the flour with the paprika and season the breadcrumbs with the remaining ½ teaspoon of salt and ½ teaspoon of pepper.
6. To bread the pork, place a pork chop in the flour, then into the whisked eggs, and then into the breadcrumbs. Place the breaded pork onto a plate and finish breading the remaining pork chops.
7. Preheat the air fryer to 390°F.
8. Place the pork chops into the air fryer, not overlapping and working in batches as needed. Spray the pork chops with cooking spray and cook for 8 minutes; flip the pork and cook for another 4 to 6 minutes or until cooked to an internal temperature of 145°F.
9. Serve with lemon wedges.

Stuffed Bell Peppers

Servings: 4

Cooking Time: 10 Minutes

Ingredients:

- ¼ pound lean ground pork
- ¾ pound lean ground beef
- ¼ cup onion, minced
- 1 15-ounce can Red Gold crushed tomatoes
- 1 teaspoon Worcestershire sauce
- 1 teaspoon barbeque seasoning
- 1 teaspoon honey
- ½ teaspoon dried basil
- ½ cup cooked brown rice
- ½ teaspoon garlic powder
- ½ teaspoon oregano
- ½ teaspoon salt
- 2 small bell peppers

Directions:

1. Place pork, beef, and onion in air fryer baking pan and cook at 360°F for 5minutes.
2. Stir to break apart chunks and cook 3 more minutes. Continue cooking and stirring in 2-minute intervals until meat is well done. Remove from pan and drain.
3. In a small saucepan, combine the tomatoes, Worcestershire, barbeque seasoning, honey, and basil. Stir well to mix in honey and seasonings.
4. In a large bowl, combine the cooked meat mixture, rice, garlic powder, oregano, and salt. Add ¼ cup of the seasoned crushed tomatoes. Stir until well mixed.
5. Cut peppers in half and remove stems and seeds.
6. Stuff each pepper half with one fourth of the meat mixture.
7. Place the peppers in air fryer basket and cook for 10 minutes, until peppers are crisp tender.
8. Heat remaining tomato sauce. Serve peppers with warm sauce spooned over top.

Pork & Beef Egg Rolls

Servings: 8
Cooking Time: 8 Minutes

Ingredients:

- ¼ pound very lean ground beef
- ¼ pound lean ground pork
- 1 tablespoon soy sauce
- 1 teaspoon olive oil
- ½ cup grated carrots
- 2 green onions, chopped
- 2 cups grated Napa cabbage
- ¼ cup chopped water chestnuts
- ¼ teaspoon salt
- ¼ teaspoon garlic powder
- ¼ teaspoon black pepper
- 1 egg
- 1 tablespoon water
- 8 egg roll wraps
- oil for misting or cooking spray

Directions:

1. In a large skillet, brown beef and pork with soy sauce. Remove cooked meat from skillet, drain, and set aside.

2. Pour off any excess grease from skillet. Add olive oil, carrots, and onions. Sauté until barely tender, about 1 minute.

3. Stir in cabbage, cover, and cook for 1 minute or just until cabbage slightly wilts. Remove from heat.

4. In a large bowl, combine the cooked meats and vegetables, water chestnuts, salt, garlic powder, and pepper. Stir well. If needed, add more salt to taste.

5. Beat together egg and water in a small bowl.

6. Fill egg roll wrappers, using about ¼ cup of filling for each wrap. Roll up and brush all over with egg wash to seal. Spray very lightly with olive oil or cooking spray.

7. Place 4 egg rolls in air fryer basket and cook at 390°F for 4minutes. Turn over and cook 4 more minutes, until golden brown and crispy.

8. Repeat to cook remaining egg rolls.

Spicy Hoisin Bbq Pork Chops

Servings: 2
Cooking Time: 12 Minutes

Ingredients:

- 3 tablespoons hoisin sauce
- ¼ cup honey
- 1 tablespoon soy sauce
- 3 tablespoons rice vinegar
- 2 tablespoons brown sugar
- 1½ teaspoons grated fresh ginger
- 1 to 2 teaspoons Sriracha sauce, to taste
- 2 to 3 bone-in center cut pork chops, 1-inch thick (about 1¼ pounds)
- chopped scallions, for garnish

Directions:

1. Combine the hoisin sauce, honey, soy sauce, rice vinegar, brown sugar, ginger, and Sriracha sauce in a small saucepan. Whisk the ingredients together and bring the mixture to a boil over medium-high heat on the stovetop. Reduce the heat and simmer the sauce until it has reduced in volume and thickened slightly – about 10 minutes.

2. Preheat the air fryer to 400°F.

3. Place the pork chops into the air fryer basket and pour half the hoisin BBQ sauce over the top. Air-fry for 6 minutes. Then, flip the chops over, pour the remaining hoisin BBQ sauce on top and air-fry for 6 more minutes, depending on the thickness of the pork chops. The internal

temperature of the pork chops should be 155°F when tested with an instant read thermometer.

4. Let the pork chops rest for 5 minutes before serving. You can spoon a little of the sauce from the bottom drawer of the air fryer over the top if desired. Sprinkle with chopped scallions and serve.

Calzones South Of The Border

Servings: 8

Cooking Time: 8 Minutes

Ingredients:

- Filling
- ¼ pound ground pork sausage
- ½ teaspoon chile powder
- ¼ teaspoon ground cumin
- ⅛ teaspoon garlic powder
- ⅛ teaspoon onion powder
- ⅛ teaspoon oregano
- ½ cup ricotta cheese
- 1 ounce sharp Cheddar cheese, shredded
- 2 ounces Pepper Jack cheese, shredded
- 1 4-ounce can chopped green chiles, drained
- oil for misting or cooking spray
- salsa, sour cream, or guacamole
- Crust
- 2 cups white wheat flour, plus more for kneading and rolling
- 1 package (¼ ounce) RapidRise yeast
- 1 teaspoon salt
- ½ teaspoon chile powder
- ½ teaspoon ground cumin
- 1 cup warm water (115°F to 125°F)
- 2 teaspoons olive oil

Directions:

1. Crumble sausage into air fryer baking pan and stir in the filling seasonings: chile powder, cumin, garlic powder, onion powder, and oregano. Cook at 390°F for 2minutes. Stir, breaking apart, and cook for 3 to 4minutes, until well done. Remove and set aside on paper towels to drain.

2. To make dough, combine flour, yeast, salt, chile powder, and cumin. Stir in warm water and oil until soft dough forms. Turn out onto lightly floured board and knead for 3 or 4minutes. Let dough rest for 10minutes.

3. Place the three cheeses in a medium bowl. Add cooked sausage and chiles and stir until well mixed.

4. Cut dough into 8 pieces.

5. Working with 4 pieces of the dough, press each into a circle about 5 inches in diameter. Top each dough circle with 2 heaping tablespoons of filling. Fold over into a half-moon shape and press edges together. Seal edges firmly to prevent leakage. Spray both sides with oil or cooking spray.

6. Place 4 calzones in air fryer basket and cook at 360°F for 5minutes. Mist with oil or spray and cook for 3minutes, until crust is done and nicely browned.

7. While the first batch is cooking, press out the remaining dough, fill, and shape into calzones.

8. Spray both sides with oil or cooking spray and cook for 5minutes. If needed, mist with oil and continue cooking for 3 minutes longer. This second batch will cook a little faster than the first because your air fryer is already hot.

9. Serve plain or with salsa, sour cream, or guacamole.

Natchitoches Meat Pies

Servings: 8
Cooking Time: 12 Minutes

Ingredients:
- Filling
- ½ pound lean ground beef
- ¼ cup finely chopped onion
- ¼ cup finely chopped green bell pepper
- ⅛ teaspoon salt
- ½ teaspoon garlic powder
- ½ teaspoon red pepper flakes
- 1 tablespoon low sodium Worcestershire sauce
- Crust
- 2 cups self-rising flour
- ¼ cup butter, finely diced
- 1 cup milk
- Egg Wash
- 1 egg
- 1 tablespoon water or milk
- oil for misting or cooking spray

Directions:
1. Mix all filling ingredients well and shape into 4 small patties.
2. Cook patties in air fryer basket at 390°F for 10 to 12minutes or until well done.
3. Place patties in large bowl and use fork and knife to crumble meat into very small pieces. Set aside.
4. To make the crust, use a pastry blender or fork to cut the butter into the flour until well mixed. Add milk and stir until dough stiffens.
5. Divide dough into 8 equal portions.
6. On a lightly floured surface, roll each portion of dough into a circle. The circle should be thin and about 5 inches in diameter, but don't worry about getting a perfect shape. Uneven circles result in a rustic look that many people prefer.
7. Spoon 2 tablespoons of meat filling onto each dough circle.
8. Brush egg wash all the way around the edge of dough circle, about ½-inch deep.
9. Fold each circle in half and press dough with tines of a dinner fork to seal the edges all the way around.
10. Brush tops of sealed meat pies with egg wash.
11. Cook filled pies in a single layer in air fryer basket at 360°F for 4minutes. Spray tops with oil or cooking spray, turn pies over, and spray bottoms with oil or cooking spray. Cook for an additional 2minutes.
12. Repeat previous step to cook remaining pies.

Pepperoni Pockets

Servings: 4
Cooking Time: 8 Minutes

Ingredients:
- 4 bread slices, 1-inch thick
- olive oil for misting
- 24 slices pepperoni (about 2 ounces)
- 1 ounce roasted red peppers, drained and patted dry
- 1 ounce Pepper Jack cheese cut into 4 slices
- pizza sauce (optional)

Directions:
1. Spray both sides of bread slices with olive oil.
2. Stand slices upright and cut a deep slit in the top to create a pocket—almost to the bottom crust but not all the way through.
3. Stuff each bread pocket with 6 slices of pepperoni, a large strip of roasted red pepper, and a slice of cheese.

4. Place bread pockets in air fryer basket, standing up. Cook at 360°F for 8 minutes, until filling is heated through and bread is lightly browned. Serve while hot as is or with pizza sauce for dipping.

Pork Schnitzel With Dill Sauce

Servings: 4
Cooking Time: 4 Minutes

Ingredients:

- 6 boneless, center cut pork chops (about 1½ pounds)
- ½ cup flour
- 1½ teaspoons salt
- freshly ground black pepper
- 2 eggs
- ½ cup milk
- 1½ cups toasted fine breadcrumbs
- 1 teaspoon paprika
- 3 tablespoons butter, melted
- 2 tablespoons vegetable or olive oil
- lemon wedges
- Dill Sauce:
- 1 cup chicken stock
- 1½ tablespoons cornstarch
- ⅓ cup sour cream
- 1½ tablespoons chopped fresh dill
- salt and pepper

Directions:

1. Trim the excess fat from the pork chops and pound each chop with a meat mallet between two pieces of plastic wrap until they are ½-inch thick.

2. Set up a dredging station. Combine the flour, salt, and black pepper in a shallow dish. Whisk the eggs and milk together in a second shallow dish. Finally, combine the breadcrumbs and paprika in a third shallow dish.

3. Dip each flattened pork chop in the flour. Shake off the excess flour and dip each chop into the egg mixture. Finally dip them into the breadcrumbs and press the breadcrumbs onto the meat firmly. Place each finished chop on a baking sheet until they are all coated.

4. Preheat the air fryer to 400°F.

5. Combine the melted butter and the oil in a small bowl and lightly brush both sides of the coated pork chops. Do not brush the chops too heavily or the breading will not be as crispy.

6. Air-fry one schnitzel at a time for 4 minutes, turning it over halfway through the cooking time. Hold the cooked schnitzels warm on a baking pan in a 170°F oven while you finish air-frying the rest.

7. While the schnitzels are cooking, whisk the chicken stock and cornstarch together in a small saucepan over medium-high heat on the stovetop. Bring the mixture to a boil and simmer for 2 minutes. Remove the saucepan from heat and whisk in the sour cream. Add the chopped fresh dill and season with salt and pepper.

8. Transfer the pork schnitzel to a platter and serve with dill sauce and lemon wedges. For a traditional meal, serve this along side some egg noodles, spätzle or German potato salad.

APPETIZERS AND SNACKS

Classic Potato Chips

Servings: 4
Cooking Time: 8 Minutes

Ingredients:
- 2 medium russet potatoes, washed
- 2 cups filtered water
- 1 tablespoon avocado oil
- ½ teaspoon salt

Directions:
1. Using a mandolin, slice the potatoes into ⅛-inch-thick pieces.
2. Pour the water into a large bowl. Place the potatoes in the bowl and soak for at least 30 minutes.
3. Preheat the air fryer to 350°F.
4. Drain the water and pat the potatoes dry with a paper towel or kitchen cloth. Toss with avocado oil and salt. Liberally spray the air fryer basket with olive oil mist.
5. Set the potatoes inside the air fryer basket, separating them so they're not on top of each other. Cook for 5 minutes, shake the basket, and cook another 5 minutes, or until browned.
6. Remove and let cool a few minutes prior to serving. Repeat until all the chips are cooked.

Barbecue Chicken Nachos

Servings: 3
Cooking Time: 5 Minutes

Ingredients:
- 3 heaping cups (a little more than 3 ounces) Corn tortilla chips (gluten-free, if a concern)
- ¾ cup Shredded deboned and skinned rotisserie chicken meat (gluten-free, if a concern)
- 3 tablespoons Canned black beans, drained and rinsed
- 9 rings Pickled jalapeño slices
- 4 Small pickled cocktail onions, halved
- 3 tablespoons Barbecue sauce (any sort)
- ¾ cup (about 3 ounces) Shredded Cheddar cheese

Directions:
1. Preheat the air fryer to 400°F.
2. Cut a circle of parchment paper to line a 6-inch round cake pan for a small air fryer, a 7-inch round cake pan for a medium air fryer, or an 8-inch round cake pan for a large machine.
3. Fill the pan with an even layer of about two-thirds of the chips. Sprinkle the chicken evenly over the chips. Set the pan in the basket and air-fry undisturbed for 2 minutes.
4. Remove the basket from the machine. Scatter the beans, jalapeño rings, and pickled onion halves over the chicken. Drizzle the barbecue sauce over everything, then sprinkle the cheese on top.
5. Return the basket to the machine and air-fry undisturbed for 3 minutes, or until the cheese has melted and is bubbly. Remove the pan from the machine and cool for a couple of minutes before serving.

Pizza Bagel Bites

Servings: 2
Cooking Time: 5 Minutes

Ingredients:
- 2 Mini bagel(s), split into two rings
- ¼ cup Purchased pizza sauce
- ½ cup Finely grated or shredded cheese, such as Parmesan cheese, semi-firm mozzarella, fontina, or (preferably) a cheese blend

Directions:
1. Preheat the air fryer to 375°F .
2. Spread the cut side of each bagel half with 1 tablespoon pizza sauce; top each half with 2 tablespoons shredded cheese.
3. When the machine is at temperature, put the bagels cheese side up in the basket in one layer. Air-fry undisturbed for 4 minutes, or until the cheese has melted and is gooey. You may need to air-fry the pizza bagel bites for 1 minute extra if the temperature is at 360°F.
4. Use a nonstick-safe spatula to transfer the topped bagel halves to a wire rack. Cool for at least 5 minutes before serving.

Fried Peaches

Servings: 4
Cooking Time: 8 Minutes

Ingredients:
- 2 egg whites
- 1 tablespoon water
- ¼ cup sliced almonds
- 2 tablespoons brown sugar
- ½ teaspoon almond extract
- 1 cup crisp rice cereal
- 2 medium, very firm peaches, peeled and pitted
- ¼ cup cornstarch
- oil for misting or cooking spray

Directions:
1. Preheat air fryer to 390°F.
2. Beat together egg whites and water in a shallow dish.
3. In a food processor, combine the almonds, brown sugar, and almond extract. Process until ingredients combine well and the nuts are finely chopped.
4. Add cereal and pulse just until cereal crushes. Pour crumb mixture into a shallow dish or onto a plate.
5. Cut each peach into eighths and place in a plastic bag or container with lid. Add cornstarch, seal, and shake to coat.
6. Remove peach slices from bag or container, tapping them hard to shake off the excess cornstarch. Dip in egg wash and roll in crumbs. Spray with oil.
7. Place in air fryer basket and cook for 5minutes. Shake basket, separate any that have stuck together, and spritz a little oil on any spots that aren't browning.
8. Cook for 3 minutes longer, until golden brown and crispy.

Sweet-and-salty Pretzels

Servings: 4
Cooking Time: 5 Minutes

Ingredients:
- 2 cups Plain pretzel nuggets
- 1 tablespoon Worcestershire sauce
- 2 teaspoons Granulated white sugar
- 1 teaspoon Mild smoked paprika
- ½ teaspoon Garlic or onion powder

Directions:

1. Preheat the air fryer to 350°F .

2. Put the pretzel nuggets, Worcestershire sauce, sugar, smoked paprika, and garlic or onion powder in a large bowl. Toss gently until the nuggets are well coated.

3. When the machine is at temperature, pour the nuggets into the basket, spreading them into as close to a single layer as possible. Air-fry, shaking the basket three or four times to rearrange the nuggets, for 5 minutes, or until the nuggets are toasted and aromatic. Although the coating will darken, don't let it burn, especially if the machine's temperature is 360°F.

4. Pour the nuggets onto a wire rack and gently spread them into one layer. (A rubber spatula does a good job.) Cool for 5 minutes before serving.

Herbed Cheese Brittle

Servings: 4
Cooking Time: 5 Minutes

Ingredients:
- ½ cup shredded Parmesan cheese
- ½ cup shredded white cheddar cheese
- 1 tablespoon fresh chopped rosemary
- 1 teaspoon garlic powder
- 1 large egg white

Directions:
1. Preheat the air fryer to 400°F.

2. In a large bowl, mix the cheeses, rosemary, and garlic powder. Mix in the egg white. Then pour the batter into a 7-inch pan (or an air-fryer-compatible pan). Place the pan in the air fryer basket and cook for 4 to 5 minutes, or until the cheese is melted and slightly browned.

3. Remove the pan from the air fryer, and let it cool for 2 minutes. Invert the pan before the cheese brittle completely cools but is semi-hardened to allow it to easily slide out of the pan.

4. Let the pan cool another 5 minutes. Break into pieces and serve.

Buffalo Wings

Servings: 2
Cooking Time: 12 Minutes Per Batch

Ingredients:
- 2 pounds chicken wings
- 3 tablespoons butter, melted
- ¼ cup hot sauce (like Crystal® or Frank's®)
- Finishing Sauce:
- 3 tablespoons butter, melted
- ¼ cup hot sauce (like Crystal® or Frank's®)
- 1 teaspoon Worcestershire sauce

Directions:
1. Prepare the chicken wings by cutting off the wing tips and discarding (or freezing for chicken stock). Divide the drumettes from the wingettes by cutting through the joint. Place the chicken wing pieces in a large bowl.

2. Combine the melted butter and the hot sauce and stir to blend well. Pour the marinade over the chicken wings, cover and let the wings marinate for 2 hours or up to overnight in the refrigerator.

3. Preheat the air fryer to 400°F.

4. Air-fry the wings in two batches for 10 minutes per batch, shaking the basket halfway through the cooking process. When both batches are done, toss all the wings back into the basket for another 2 minutes to heat through and finish cooking.

5. While the wings are air-frying, combine the remaining 3 tablespoons of butter, ¼ cup of hot sauce and the Worcestershire sauce. Remove the wings from the air fryer, toss them in the finishing sauce and serve with some cooling blue cheese dip and celery sticks.

Rumaki

Servings: 24
Cooking Time: 12 Minutes

Ingredients:

- 10 ounces raw chicken livers
- 1 can sliced water chestnuts, drained
- ¼ cup low-sodium teriyaki sauce
- 12 slices turkey bacon
- toothpicks

Directions:

1. Cut livers into 1½-inch pieces, trimming out tough veins as you slice.
2. Place livers, water chestnuts, and teriyaki sauce in small container with lid. If needed, add another tablespoon of teriyaki sauce to make sure livers are covered. Refrigerate for 1 hour.
3. When ready to cook, cut bacon slices in half crosswise.
4. Wrap 1 piece of liver and 1 slice of water chestnut in each bacon strip. Secure with toothpick.
5. When you have wrapped half of the livers, place them in the air fryer basket in a single layer.
6. Cook at 390°F for 12 minutes, until liver is done and bacon is crispy.
7. While first batch cooks, wrap the remaining livers. Repeat step 6 to cook your second batch.

Bacon Candy

Servings: 6
Cooking Time: 6 Minutes

Ingredients:

- 1½ tablespoons Honey
- 1 teaspoon White wine vinegar
- 3 Extra thick–cut bacon strips, halved widthwise (gluten-free, if a concern)
- ½ teaspoon Ground black pepper

Directions:

1. Preheat the air fryer to 350°F .
2. Whisk the honey and vinegar in a small bowl until incorporated.
3. When the machine is at temperature, remove the basket. Lay the bacon strip halves in the basket in one layer. Brush the tops with the honey mixture; sprinkle each bacon strip evenly with black pepper.
4. Return the basket to the machine and air-fry undisturbed for 6 minutes, or until the bacon is crunchy. Or a little less time if you prefer bacon that's still pliable, an extra minute if you want the bacon super crunchy. Take care that the honey coating doesn't burn. Remove the basket from the machine and set aside for 5 minutes. Use kitchen tongs to transfer the bacon strips to a serving plate.

Roasted Chickpeas

Servings: 1
Cooking Time: 15 Minutes

Ingredients:

- 1 15-ounce can chickpeas, drained
- 2 teaspoons curry powder
- ¼ teaspoon salt
- 1 tablespoon olive oil

Directions:

1. Drain chickpeas thoroughly and spread in a single layer on paper towels. Cover with another paper towel and press gently to remove extra moisture. Don't press too hard or you'll crush the chickpeas.
2. Mix curry powder and salt together.
3. Place chickpeas in a medium bowl and sprinkle with seasonings. Stir well to coat.

4. Add olive oil and stir again to distribute oil.

5. Cook at 390°F for 15minutes, stopping to shake basket about halfway through cooking time.

6. Cool completely and store in airtight container.

Crabby Fries

Servings: 2

Cooking Time: 30 Minutes

Ingredients:

- 2 to 3 large russet potatoes, peeled and cut into ½-inch sticks
- 2 tablespoons vegetable oil
- 2 tablespoons butter
- 2 tablespoons flour
- 1 to 1½ cups milk
- ½ cup grated white Cheddar cheese
- pinch of nutmeg
- ½ teaspoon salt
- freshly ground black pepper
- 1 tablespoon Old Bay® Seasoning

Directions:

1. Bring a large saucepan of salted water to a boil on the stovetop while you peel and cut the potatoes. Blanch the potatoes in the boiling salted water for 4 minutes while you Preheat the air fryer to 400°F. Strain the potatoes and rinse them with cold water. Dry them well with a clean kitchen towel.

2. Toss the dried potato sticks gently with the oil and place them in the air fryer basket. Air-fry for 25 minutes, shaking the basket a few times while the fries cook to help them brown evenly.

3. While the fries are cooking, melt the butter in a medium saucepan. Whisk in the flour and cook for one minute. Slowly add 1 cup of milk, whisking constantly. Bring the mixture to a simmer and continue to whisk until it thickens. Remove the pan from the heat and stir in the Cheddar cheese. Add a pinch of nutmeg and season with salt and freshly ground black pepper. Transfer the warm cheese sauce to a serving dish. Thin with more milk if you want the sauce a little thinner.

4. As soon as the French fries have finished air-frying transfer them to a large bowl and season them with the Old Bay® Seasoning. Return the fries to the air fryer basket and air-fry for an additional 3 to 5 minutes. Serve immediately with the warm white Cheddar cheese sauce.

Charred Shishito Peppers

Servings: 4

Cooking Time: 5 Minutes

Ingredients:

- 20 shishito peppers (about 6 ounces)
- 1 teaspoon vegetable oil
- coarse sea salt
- 1 lemon

Directions:

1. Preheat the air fryer to 390°F.

2. Toss the shishito peppers with the oil and salt. You can do this in a bowl or directly in the air fryer basket.

3. Air-fry at 390°F for 5 minutes, shaking the basket once or twice while they cook.

4. Turn the charred peppers out into a bowl. Squeeze some lemon juice over the top and season with coarse sea salt. These should be served as finger foods – pick the pepper up by the stem and eat the whole pepper, seeds and all. Watch for that surprise spicy one!

Avocado Egg Rolls

Servings: 8
Cooking Time: 8 Minutes

Ingredients:

- 8 full-size egg roll wrappers
- 1 medium avocado, sliced into 8 pieces
- 1 cup cooked black beans, divided
- ½ cup mild salsa, divided
- ½ cup shredded Mexican cheese, divided
- ⅓ cup filtered water, divided
- ½ cup sour cream
- 1 teaspoon chipotle hot sauce

Directions:

1. Preheat the air fryer to 400°F.
2. Place the egg roll wrapper on a flat surface and place 1 strip of avocado down in the center.
3. Top the avocado with 2 tablespoons of black beans, 1 tablespoon of salsa, and 1 tablespoon of shredded cheese.
4. Place two of your fingers into the water, and then moisten the four outside edges of the egg roll wrapper with water (so the outer edges will secure shut).
5. Fold the bottom corner up, covering the filling. Then secure the sides over the top, remembering to lightly moisten them so they stick. Tightly roll the egg roll up and moisten the final flap of the wrapper and firmly press it into the egg roll to secure it shut.
6. Repeat Steps 2–5 until all 8 egg rolls are complete.
7. When ready to cook, spray the air fryer basket with olive oil spray and place the egg rolls into the basket. Depending on the size and type of air fryer you have, you may need to do this in two sets.
8. Cook for 4 minutes, flip, and then cook the remaining 4 minutes.
9. Repeat until all the egg rolls are cooked. Meanwhile, mix the sour cream with the hot sauce to serve as a dipping sauce.
10. Serve warm.

Onion Ring Nachos

Servings: 3
Cooking Time: 8 Minutes

Ingredients:

- ¾ pound Frozen breaded (not battered) onion rings (do not thaw)
- 1½ cups (about 6 ounces) Shredded Cheddar, Monterey Jack, or Swiss cheese, or a purchased Tex-Mex blend
- Up to 12 Pickled jalapeño rings

Directions:

1. Preheat the air fryer to 400°F.
2. When the machine is at temperature, spread the onion rings in the basket in a fairly even layer. Air-fry undisturbed for 6 minutes, or until crisp. Remove the basket from the machine.
3. Cut a circle of parchment paper to line a 6-inch round cake pan for a small air fryer, a 7-inch round cake pan for a medium air fryer, or an 8-inch round cake pan for a large machine.
4. Pour the onion rings into a fairly even layer in the cake pan, then sprinkle the cheese evenly over them. Dot with the jalapeño rings.
5. Set the pan in the basket and air-fry undisturbed for 2 minutes, until the cheese has melted and is bubbling.
6. Remove the pan from the basket. Cool for 5 minutes before serving.

Sweet Plantain Chips

Servings: 4
Cooking Time: 11 Minutes

Ingredients:

- 2 Very ripe plantain(s), peeled and sliced into 1-inch pieces
- Vegetable oil spray
- 3 tablespoons Maple syrup
- For garnishing Coarse sea salt or kosher salt

Directions:

1. Pour about ½ cup water into the bottom of your air fryer basket or into a metal tray on a lower rack in some models. Preheat the air fryer to 400°F.

2. Put the plantain pieces in a bowl, coat them with vegetable oil spray, and toss gently, spraying at least one more time and tossing repeatedly, until the pieces are well coated.

3. When the machine is at temperature, arrange the plantain pieces in the basket in one layer. Air-fry undisturbed for 5 minutes.

4. Remove the basket from the machine and spray the back of a metal spatula with vegetable oil spray. Use the spatula to press down on the plantain pieces, spraying it again as needed, to flatten the pieces to about half their original height. Brush the plantain pieces with maple syrup, then return the basket to the machine and continue air-frying undisturbed for 6 minutes, or until the plantain pieces are soft and caramelized.

5. Use kitchen tongs to transfer the pieces to a serving platter. Sprinkle the pieces with salt and cool for a couple of minutes before serving. Or cool to room temperature before serving, about 1 hour.

Smoked Whitefish Spread

Servings: 1
Cooking Time: 10 Minutes

Ingredients:

- ¾ pound Boneless skinless white-flesh fish fillets, such as hake or trout
- 3 tablespoons Liquid smoke
- 3 tablespoons Regular, low-fat, or fat-free mayonnaise (gluten-free, if a concern)
- 2 teaspoons Jarred prepared white horseradish (optional)
- ¼ teaspoon Onion powder
- ¼ teaspoon Celery seeds
- ¼ teaspoon Table salt
- ¼ teaspoon Ground black pepper

Directions:

1. Put the fish fillets in a zip-closed bag, add the liquid smoke, and seal closed. Rub the liquid smoke all over the fish , then refrigerate the sealed bag for 2 hours.

2. Preheat the air fryer to 400°F.

3. Set a 12-inch piece of aluminum foil on your work surface. Remove the fish fillets from the bag and set them in the center of this piece of foil (the fillets can overlap). Fold the long sides of the foil together and crimp them closed. Make a tight seam so no steam can escape. Fold up the ends and crimp to seal well.

4. Set the packet in the basket and air-fry undisturbed for 10 minutes.

5. Use kitchen tongs to transfer the foil packet to a wire rack. Cool for a minute or so. Open the packet, transfer the fish to a plate, and refrigerate for 30 minutes.

6. Put the cold fish in a food processor. Add the mayonnaise, horseradish (if using), onion powder,

celery seeds, salt, and pepper. Cover and pulse to a slightly coarse spread, certainly not fully smooth.

7. For a more traditional texture, put the fish fillets in a bowl, add the other ingredients, and stir with a wooden spoon, mashing the fish with everything else to make a coarse paste.

8. Scrape the spread into a bowl and serve at once, or cover with plastic wrap and store in the fridge for up to 4 days.

Individual Pizzas

Servings: 2
Cooking Time: 7 Minutes

Ingredients:
- 6 ounces Purchased fresh pizza dough (not a prebaked crust)
- Olive oil spray
- 4½ tablespoons Purchased pizza sauce or purchased pesto
- ½ cup (about 2 ounces) Shredded semi-firm mozzarella

Directions:
1. Preheat the air fryer to 400°F.
2. Press the pizza dough into a 5-inch circle for a small air fryer, a 6-inch circle for a medium air fryer, or a 7-inch circle for a large machine. Generously coat the top of the dough with olive oil spray.
3. Remove the basket from the machine and set the dough oil side down in the basket. Smear the sauce or pesto over the dough, then sprinkle with the cheese.
4. Return the basket to the machine and air-fry undisturbed for 7 minutes, or until the dough is puffed and browned and the cheese has melted. (Extra toppings will not increase the cooking time, provided you add no extra cheese.)

5. Remove the basket from the machine and cool the pizza in it for 5 minutes. Use a large nonstick-safe spatula to transfer the pizza from the basket to a wire rack. Cool for 5 minutes more before serving.

Eggplant Fries

Servings: 4
Cooking Time: 8 Minutes

Ingredients:
- 1 medium eggplant
- 1 teaspoon ground coriander
- 1 teaspoon cumin
- 1 teaspoon garlic powder
- ½ teaspoon salt
- 1 cup crushed panko breadcrumbs
- 1 large egg
- 2 tablespoons water
- oil for misting or cooking spray

Directions:
1. Peel and cut the eggplant into fat fries, ⅜- to ½-inch thick.
2. Preheat air fryer to 390°F.
3. In a small cup, mix together the coriander, cumin, garlic, and salt.
4. Combine 1 teaspoon of the seasoning mix and panko crumbs in a shallow dish.
5. Place eggplant fries in a large bowl, sprinkle with remaining seasoning, and stir well to combine.
6. Beat eggs and water together and pour over eggplant fries. Stir to coat.
7. Remove eggplant from egg wash, shaking off excess, and roll in panko crumbs.
8. Spray with oil.

9. Place half of the fries in air fryer basket. You should have only a single layer, but it's fine if they overlap a little.

10. Cook for 5minutes. Shake basket, mist lightly with oil, and cook 3 minutes longer, until browned and crispy.

11. Repeat step 10 to cook remaining eggplant.

Thick-crust Pepperoni Pizza

Servings: 2
Cooking Time: 10 Minutes

Ingredients:

- 10 ounces Purchased fresh pizza dough (not a prebaked crust)
- Olive oil spray
- ¼ cup Purchased pizza sauce
- 10 slices Sliced pepperoni
- ⅓ cup Purchased shredded Italian 3- or 4- cheese blend

Directions:

1. Preheat the air fryer to 400°F.

2. Generously coat the inside of a 6-inch round cake pan for a small air fryer, a 7-inch round cake pan for a medium air fryer, or an 8-inch round cake pan for a large model with olive oil spray.

3. Set the dough in the pan and press it to fill the bottom in an even, thick layer. Spread the sauce over the dough, then top with the pepperoni and cheese.

4. When the machine is at temperature, set the pan in the basket and air-fry undisturbed for 10 minutes, or until puffed, brown, and bubbling.

5. Use kitchen tongs to transfer the cake pan to a wire rack. Cool for only a minute or so. Use a spatula to loosen the pizza from the pan and lift it out and onto the rack. Continue cooling for a few minutes before cutting into wedges to serve.

Spiced Nuts

Servings: 3
Cooking Time: 25 Minutes

Ingredients:

- 1 egg white, lightly beaten
- ¼ cup sugar
- 1 teaspoon salt
- ½ teaspoon ground cinnamon
- ¼ teaspoon ground cloves
- ¼ teaspoon ground allspice
- pinch ground cayenne pepper
- 1 cup pecan halves
- 1 cup cashews
- 1 cup almonds

Directions:

1. Combine the egg white with the sugar and spices in a bowl.

2. Preheat the air fryer to 300°F.

3. Spray or brush the air fryer basket with vegetable oil. Toss the nuts together in the spiced egg white and transfer the nuts to the air fryer basket.

4. Air-fry for 25 minutes, stirring the nuts in the basket a few times during the cooking process. Taste the nuts to see if they are crunchy and nicely toasted. Air-fry for a few more minutes if necessary.

5. Serve warm or cool to room temperature and store in an airtight container for up to two weeks.

Turkey Bacon Dates

Servings: 16
Cooking Time: 7 Minutes

Ingredients:

- 16 whole, pitted dates
- 16 whole almonds

- 6 to 8 strips turkey bacon

Directions:

1.   Stuff each date with a whole almond.

2.   Depending on the size of your stuffed dates, cut bacon strips into halves or thirds. Each strip should be long enough to wrap completely around a date.

3.   Wrap each date in a strip of bacon with ends overlapping and secure with toothpicks.

4.   Place in air fryer basket and cook at 390°F for 7 minutes, until bacon is as crispy as you like.

5.   Drain on paper towels or wire rack. Serve hot or at room temperature.

Savory Sausage Balls

Servings: 10
Cooking Time: 8 Minutes

Ingredients:

- 2 cups all-purpose flour
- 1 tablespoon baking powder
- ½ teaspoon garlic powder
- ¼ teaspoon onion powder
- ½ teaspoon salt
- 3 tablespoons milk
- 2½ cups grated pepper jack cheese
- 1 pound fresh sausage, casing removed

Directions:

1.   Preheat the air fryer to 370°F.

2.   In a large bowl, whisk together the flour, baking powder, garlic powder, onion powder, and salt. Add in the milk, grated cheese, and sausage.

3.   Using a tablespoon, scoop out the sausage and roll it between your hands to form a rounded ball. You should end up with approximately 32 balls. Place them in the air fryer basket in a single layer and working in batches as necessary.

4.   Cook for 8 minutes, or until the outer coating turns light brown.

5.   Carefully remove, repeating with the remaining sausage balls.

Vegetable Spring Rolls

Servings: 6
Cooking Time: 8 Minutes

Ingredients:

- ¾ cup (a little more than 2½ ounces) Fresh bean sprouts
- 6 tablespoons Shredded carrots
- 6 tablespoons Slivered, drained, sliced canned bamboo shoots
- 1½ tablespoons Regular or low-sodium soy sauce or gluten-free tamari sauce
- 1½ teaspoons Granulated white sugar
- 1½ teaspoons Toasted sesame oil
- 6 Spring roll wrappers (gluten-free, if a concern)
- 1 Large egg, well beaten
- Vegetable oil spray

Directions:

1.   Gently stir the bean sprouts, carrots, bamboo shoots, soy or tamari sauce, sugar, and oil in a large bowl until the vegetables are evenly coated. Set aside at room temperature for 10 to 15 minutes.

2.   Preheat the air fryer to 400°F.

3.   Set a spring roll wrapper on a clean, dry work surface. Pick up about ¼ cup of the vegetable mixture and gently squeeze it in your clean hand to release most of the liquid. Set this bundle of vegetables along one edge of the wrapper.

4.   Fold two opposing sides (at right angles to the filling) up and over the filling, concealing part of it and making a folded-over border down two

sides of the wrapper. Brush the top half of the wrapper (including the folded parts) with beaten egg so it will seal when you roll it closed.

5. Starting with the side nearest the filling, roll the wrapper closed, working to make a tight fit, eliminating as much air as possible from inside the wrapper. Set it aside seam side down and continue making more filled rolls using the same techniques.

6. Lightly coat all the sealed rolls with vegetable oil spray on all sides. Set them seam side down in the basket and air-fry undisturbed for 8 minutes, or until golden brown and very crisp.

7. Use a nonstick-safe spatula and a flatware fork for balance to transfer the rolls to a wire rack. Cool for at least 5 minutes or up to 15 minutes before serving.

Buffalo Bites

Servings: 16
Cooking Time: 12 Minutes

Ingredients:
- 1 pound ground chicken
- 8 tablespoons buffalo wing sauce
- 2 ounces Gruyère cheese, cut into 16 cubes
- 1 tablespoon maple syrup

Directions:
1. Mix 4 tablespoons buffalo wing sauce into all the ground chicken.

2. Shape chicken into a log and divide into 16 equal portions.

3. With slightly damp hands, mold each chicken portion around a cube of cheese and shape into a firm ball. When you have shaped 8 meatballs, place them in air fryer basket.

4. Cook at 390°F for approximately 5minutes. Shake basket, reduce temperature to 360°F, and cook for 5 minutes longer.

5. While the first batch is cooking, shape remaining chicken and cheese into 8 more meatballs.

6. Repeat step 4 to cook second batch of meatballs.

7. In a medium bowl, mix the remaining 4 tablespoons of buffalo wing sauce with the maple syrup. Add all the cooked meatballs and toss to coat.

8. Place meatballs back into air fryer basket and cook at 390°F for 2 minutes to set the glaze. Skewer each with a toothpick and serve.

Fried Brie With Cherry Tomatoes

Servings: 8
Cooking Time: 15 Minutes

Ingredients:
- 1 baguette*
- 2 pints red and yellow cherry tomatoes
- 1 tablespoon olive oil
- salt and freshly ground black pepper
- 1 teaspoon balsamic vinegar
- 1 tablespoon chopped fresh parsley
- 1 (8-ounce) wheel of Brie cheese
- olive oil
- ½ teaspoon Italian seasoning (optional)
- 1 tablespoon chopped fresh basil

Directions:
1. Preheat the air fryer to 350°F.

2. Start by making the crostini. Slice the baguette diagonally into ½-inch slices and brush the slices with olive oil on both sides. Air-fry the baguette slices at 350°F in batches for 6 minutes

or until lightly browned on all sides. Set the bread aside on your serving platter.

3. Toss the cherry tomatoes in a bowl with the olive oil, salt and pepper. Air-fry the cherry tomatoes for 3 to 5 minutes, shaking the basket a few times during the cooking process. The tomatoes should be soft and some of them will burst open. Toss the warm tomatoes with the balsamic vinegar and fresh parsley and set aside.

4. Cut a circle of parchment paper the same size as your wheel of Brie cheese. Brush both sides of the Brie wheel with olive oil and sprinkle with Italian seasoning, if using. Place the circle of parchment paper on one side of the Brie and transfer the Brie to the air fryer basket, parchment side down. Air-fry at 350°F for 8 to 10 minutes, or until the Brie is slightly puffed and soft to the touch.

5. Watch carefully and remove the Brie before the rind cracks and the cheese starts to leak out. Transfer the wheel to your serving platter and top with the roasted tomatoes. Sprinkle with basil and serve with the toasted bread slices.

VEGETABLE SIDE DISHES RECIPES

Roasted Garlic And Thyme Tomatoes

Servings: 2
Cooking Time: 15 Minutes

Ingredients:

- 4 Roma tomatoes
- 1 tablespoon olive oil
- salt and freshly ground black pepper
- 1 clove garlic, minced
- ½ teaspoon dried thyme

Directions:

1. Preheat the air fryer to 390°F.
2. Cut the tomatoes in half and scoop out the seeds and any pithy parts with your fingers. Place the tomatoes in a bowl and toss with the olive oil, salt, pepper, garlic and thyme.
3. Transfer the tomatoes to the air fryer, cut side up. Air-fry for 15 minutes. The edges should just start to brown. Let the tomatoes cool to an edible temperature for a few minutes and then use in pastas, on top of crostini, or as an accompaniment to any poultry, meat or fish.

Mushrooms, Sautéed

Servings: 4
Cooking Time: 4 Minutes

Ingredients:

- 8 ounces sliced white mushrooms, rinsed and well drained
- ¼ teaspoon garlic powder
- 1 tablespoon Worcestershire sauce

Directions:

1. Place mushrooms in a large bowl and sprinkle with garlic powder and Worcestershire. Stir well to distribute seasonings evenly.
2. Place in air fryer basket and cook at 390°F for 4 minutes, until tender.

Crispy Brussels Sprouts

Servings: 3
Cooking Time: 12 Minutes

Ingredients:

- 1¼ pounds Medium, 2-inch-in-length Brussels sprouts
- 1½ tablespoons Olive oil
- ¾ teaspoon Table salt

Directions:

1. Preheat the air fryer to 400°F.
2. Halve each Brussels sprout through the stem end, pulling off and discarding any discolored outer leaves. Put the sprout halves in a large bowl, add the oil and salt, and stir well to coat evenly, until the Brussels sprouts are glistening.
3. When the machine is at temperature, scrape the contents of the bowl into the basket, gently spreading the Brussels sprout halves into as close to one layer as possible. Air-fry for 12 minutes, gently tossing and rearranging the vegetables twice to get all covered or touching parts exposed to the air currents, until crisp and browned at the edges.
4. Gently pour the contents of the basket onto a wire rack. Cool for a minute or two before serving.

Rosemary Roasted Potatoes With Lemon

Servings: 4
Cooking Time: 12 Minutes

Ingredients:

- 1 pound small red-skinned potatoes, halved or cut into bite-sized chunks
- 1 tablespoon olive oil
- 1 teaspoon finely chopped fresh rosemary
- ¼ teaspoon salt
- freshly ground black pepper
- 1 tablespoon lemon zest

Directions:

1. Preheat the air fryer to 400°F.
2. Toss the potatoes with the olive oil, rosemary, salt and freshly ground black pepper.
3. Air-fry for 12 minutes (depending on the size of the chunks), tossing the potatoes a few times throughout the cooking process.
4. As soon as the potatoes are tender to a knifepoint, toss them with the lemon zest and more salt if desired.

Stuffed Onions

Servings: 6
Cooking Time: 27 Minutes

Ingredients:

- 6 Small 3½- to 4-ounce yellow or white onions
- Olive oil spray
- 6 ounces Bulk sweet Italian sausage meat (gluten-free, if a concern)
- 9 Cherry tomatoes, chopped
- 3 tablespoons Seasoned Italian-style dried bread crumbs (gluten-free, if a concern)
- 3 tablespoons (about ½ ounce) Finely grated Parmesan cheese

Directions:

1. Preheat the air fryer to 325°F (or 330°F, if that's the closest setting).
2. Cut just enough off the root ends of the onions so they will stand up on a cutting board when this end is turned down. Carefully peel off just the brown, papery skin. Now cut the top quarter off each and place the onion back on the cutting board with this end facing up. Use a flatware spoon (preferably a serrated grapefruit spoon) or a melon baller to scoop out the "insides" (interior layers) of the onion, leaving enough of the bottom and side walls so that the onion does not collapse. Depending on the thickness of the layers in the onion, this may be one or two of those layers—or even three, if they're very thin.
3. Coat the insides and outsides of the onions with olive oil spray. Set the onion "shells" in the basket and air-fry for 15 minutes.
4. Meanwhile, make the filling. Set a medium skillet over medium heat for a couple of minutes, then crumble in the sausage meat. Cook, stirring often, until browned, about 4 minutes. Transfer the contents of the skillet to a medium bowl (leave the fat behind in the skillet or add it to the bowl, depending on your cross-trainer regimen). Stir in the tomatoes, bread crumbs, and cheese until well combined.
5. When the onions are ready, use a nonstick-safe spatula to gently transfer them to a cutting board. Increase the air fryer's temperature to 350°F .
6. Pack the sausage mixture into the onion shells, gently compacting the filling and mounding it up at the top.

7. When the machine is at temperature, set the onions stuffing side up in the basket with at least ¼ inch between them. Air-fry for 12 minutes, or until lightly browned and sizzling hot.

8. Use a nonstick-safe spatula, and perhaps a flatware fork for balance, to transfer the onions to a cutting board or serving platter. Cool for 5 minutes before serving.

Green Beans

Servings: 4
Cooking Time: 12 Minutes

Ingredients:
- 1 pound fresh green beans
- 2 tablespoons Italian salad dressing
- salt and pepper

Directions:
1. Wash beans and snap off stem ends.
2. In a large bowl, toss beans with Italian dressing.
3. Cook at 330°F for 5minutes. Shake basket or stir and cook 5minutes longer. Shake basket again and, if needed, continue cooking for 2 minutes, until as tender as you like. Beans should shrivel slightly and brown in places.
4. Sprinkle with salt and pepper to taste.

Spicy Fried Green Beans

Servings: 2
Cooking Time: 8 Minutes

Ingredients:
- 12 ounces green beans, trimmed
- 2 small dried hot red chili peppers (like árbol)
- ¼ cup panko breadcrumbs
- 1 tablespoon olive oil
- ½ teaspoon salt
- ⅛ teaspoon crushed red pepper flakes
- 2 scallions, thinly sliced

Directions:
1. Preheat the air fryer to 400°F.
2. Toss the green beans, chili peppers and panko breadcrumbs with the olive oil, salt and crushed red pepper flakes.
3. Air-fry for 8 minutes (depending on the size of the beans), shaking the basket once during the cooking process. The crumbs will fall into the bottom drawer – don't worry.
4. Transfer the green beans to a serving dish, sprinkle the scallions and the toasted crumbs from the air fryer drawer on top and serve. The dried peppers are not to be eaten, but they do look nice with the green beans. You can leave them in, or take them out as you please.

Roasted Ratatouille Vegetables

Servings: 2
Cooking Time: 15 Minutes

Ingredients:
- 1 baby or Japanese eggplant, cut into 1½-inch cubes
- 1 red pepper, cut into 1-inch chunks
- 1 yellow pepper, cut into 1-inch chunks
- 1 zucchini, cut into 1-inch chunks
- 1 clove garlic, minced
- ½ teaspoon dried basil
- 1 tablespoon olive oil
- salt and freshly ground black pepper
- ¼ cup sliced sun-dried tomatoes in oil
- 2 tablespoons chopped fresh basil

Directions:
1. Preheat the air fryer to 400°F.
2. Toss the eggplant, peppers and zucchini with the garlic, dried basil, olive oil, salt and freshly ground black pepper.

3. Air-fry the vegetables at 400°F for 15 minutes, shaking the basket a few times during the cooking process to redistribute the ingredients.

4. As soon as the vegetables are tender, toss them with the sliced sun-dried tomatoes and fresh basil and serve.

Smashed Fried Baby Potatoes

Servings: 3

Cooking Time: 18 Minutes

Ingredients:

* 1½ pounds baby red or baby Yukon gold potatoes
* ¼ cup butter, melted
* 1 teaspoon olive oil
* ½ teaspoon paprika
* 1 teaspoon dried parsley
* salt and freshly ground black pepper
* 2 scallions, finely chopped

Directions:

1. Bring a large pot of salted water to a boil. Add the potatoes and boil for 18 minutes or until the potatoes are fork-tender.

2. Drain the potatoes and transfer them to a cutting board to cool slightly. Spray or brush the bottom of a drinking glass with a little oil. Smash or flatten the potatoes by pressing the glass down on each potato slowly. Try not to completely flatten the potato or smash it so hard that it breaks apart.

3. Combine the melted butter, olive oil, paprika, and parsley together.

4. Preheat the air fryer to 400°F.

5. Spray the bottom of the air fryer basket with oil and transfer one layer of the smashed potatoes into the basket. Brush with some of the butter

mixture and season generously with salt and freshly ground black pepper.

6. Air-fry at 400°F for 10 minutes. Carefully flip the potatoes over and air-fry for an additional 8 minutes until crispy and lightly browned.

7. Keep the potatoes warm in a 170°F oven or tent with aluminum foil while you cook the second batch. Sprinkle minced scallions over the potatoes and serve warm.

Charred Radicchio Salad

Servings: 4

Cooking Time: 5 Minutes

Ingredients:

* 2 Small 5- to 6-ounce radicchio head(s)
* 3 tablespoons Olive oil
* ½ teaspoon Table salt
* 2 tablespoons Balsamic vinegar
* Up to ¼ teaspoon Red pepper flakes

Directions:

1. Preheat the air fryer to 375°F .

2. Cut the radicchio head(s) into quarters through the stem end. Brush the oil over the heads, particularly getting it between the leaves along the cut sides. Sprinkle the radicchio quarters with the salt.

3. When the machine is at temperature, set the quarters cut sides up in the basket with as much air space between them as possible. They should not touch. Air-fry undisturbed for 5 minutes, watching carefully because they burn quickly, until blackened in bits and soft.

4. Use a nonstick-safe spatula to transfer the quarters to a cutting board. Cool for a minute or two, then cut out the thick stems inside the heads. Discard these tough bits and chop the remaining heads into bite-size bits. Scrape them into a bowl.

Add the vinegar and red pepper flakes. Toss well and serve warm.

Five-spice Roasted Sweet Potatoes

Servings: 4
Cooking Time: 12 Minutes

Ingredients:

- ½ teaspoon ground cinnamon
- ¼ teaspoon ground cumin
- ¼ teaspoon paprika
- 1 teaspoon chile powder
- ⅛ teaspoon turmeric
- ½ teaspoon salt (optional)
- freshly ground black pepper
- 2 large sweet potatoes, peeled and cut into ¾-inch cubes (about 3 cups)
- 1 tablespoon olive oil

Directions:

1. In a large bowl, mix together cinnamon, cumin, paprika, chile powder, turmeric, salt, and pepper to taste.
2. Add potatoes and stir well.
3. Drizzle the seasoned potatoes with the olive oil and stir until evenly coated.
4. Place seasoned potatoes in the air fryer baking pan or an ovenproof dish that fits inside your air fryer basket.
5. Cook for 6minutes at 390°F, stop, and stir well.
6. Cook for an additional 6minutes.

Chicken Salad With Sunny Citrus Dressing

Servings: 4
Cooking Time: 8 Minutes

Ingredients:

- Sunny Citrus Dressing
- 1 cup first cold-pressed extra virgin olive oil
- ⅓ cup red wine vinegar
- 2 tablespoons all natural orange marmalade
- 1 teaspoon dry mustard
- 1 teaspoon ground black pepper
- California Chicken
- 4 large chicken tenders
- 1 teaspoon olive oil
- juice of 1 small orange or clementine
- salt and pepper
- ½ teaspoon rosemary
- Salad
- 8 cups romaine or leaf lettuce, chopped or torn into bite-size pieces
- 2 clementines or small oranges, peeled and sectioned
- ½ cup dried cranberries
- 4 tablespoons sliced almonds

Directions:

1. In a 2-cup jar or container with lid, combine all dressing ingredients and shake until well blended. Refrigerate for at least 30minutes for flavors to blend.
2. Brush chicken tenders lightly with oil.
3. Drizzle orange juice over chicken.
4. Sprinkle with salt and pepper to taste.
5. Crush the rosemary and sprinkle over chicken.
6. Cook at 390°F for 3minutes, turn over, and cook for an additional 5 minutes or until chicken is tender and juices run clear.
7. When ready to serve, toss lettuce with 2 tablespoons of dressing to coat.
8. Divide lettuce among 4 plates or bowls. Arrange chicken and clementines on top and

sprinkle cranberries and almonds. Pass extra dressing at the table.

Tofu & Broccoli Salad

Servings: 4
Cooking Time: 17 Minutes

Ingredients:

- Broccoli Salad
- 4 cups fresh broccoli, cut into bite-size pieces
- ½ cup red onion, chopped
- ⅓ cup raisins or dried cherries
- ¾ cup sliced almonds
- ½ cup Asian-style salad dressing
- Tofu
- 4 ounces extra firm tofu
- 1 teaspoon smoked paprika
- 1 teaspoon onion powder
- ¼ teaspoon salt
- 2 tablespoons cornstarch
- 1 tablespoon extra virgin olive oil

Directions:

1. Place several folded paper towels on a plate and set tofu on top. Cover tofu with another folded paper towel, put another plate on top, and add heavy items such as canned goods to weigh it down. Press tofu for 30minutes.

2. While tofu is draining, combine all salad ingredients in a large bowl. Toss together well, cover, and chill until ready to serve.

3. Cut the tofu into small cubes, about ¼-inch thick. Sprinkle the cubes top and bottom with the paprika, onion powder, and salt.

4. Place cornstarch in small plastic bag, add tofu, and shake until cubes are well coated.

5. Place olive oil in another small plastic bag, add coated tofu, and shake to coat well.

6. Cook at 330°F for 17 minutes or until as crispy as you like.

7. To serve, stir chilled salad well, divide among 4 plates, and top with fried tofu.

Asiago Broccoli

Servings: 4
Cooking Time: 14 Minutes

Ingredients:

- 1 head broccoli, cut into florets
- 1 tablespoon extra-virgin olive oil
- 1 teaspoon minced garlic
- ¼ teaspoon ground black pepper
- ¼ teaspoon salt
- ¼ cup asiago cheese

Directions:

1. Preheat the air fryer to 360°F.

2. In a medium bowl, toss the broccoli florets with the olive oil, garlic, pepper, and salt. Lightly spray the air fryer basket with olive oil spray.

3. Place the broccoli florets into the basket and cook for 7 minutes. Shake the basket and sprinkle the broccoli with cheese. Cook another 7 minutes.

4. Remove from the basket and serve warm.

Roasted Broccoli And Red Bean Salad

Servings: 3
Cooking Time: 14 Minutes

Ingredients:

- 3 cups (about 1 pound) 1- to 1½-inch fresh broccoli florets (not frozen)
- 1½ tablespoons Olive oil spray
- 1¼ cups Canned red kidney beans, drained and rinsed
- 3 tablespoons Minced yellow or white onion
- 2 tablespoons plus 1 teaspoon Red wine vinegar
- ¾ teaspoon Dried oregano
- ¼ teaspoon Table salt
- ¼ teaspoon Ground black pepper

Directions:

1. Preheat the air fryer to 375°F .
2. Put the broccoli florets in a big bowl, coat them generously with olive oil spray, then toss to coat all surfaces, even down into the crannies, spraying them a couple of times more.
3. Pour the florets into the basket, spreading them into as close to one layer as you can. Air-fry for 12 minutes, tossing and rearranging the florets twice so that any touching or covered parts are eventually exposed to the air currents, until light browned but still a bit firm. (If the machine is at 360°F, you may need to add 2 minutes to the cooking time.)
4. Dump the contents of the basket onto a large cutting board. Cool for a minute or two, then chop the florets into small bits. Scrape these into a bowl and add the kidney beans, onion, vinegar, oregano, salt, and pepper. Toss well and serve warm or at room temperature.

Fried Green Tomatoes With Sriracha Mayo

Servings: 4
Cooking Time: 12 Minutes

Ingredients:

- 3 green tomatoes
- salt and freshly ground black pepper
- ⅓ cup all-purpose flour*
- 2 eggs
- ½ cup buttermilk
- 1 cup panko breadcrumbs*
- 1 cup cornmeal
- olive oil, in a spray bottle
- fresh thyme sprigs or chopped fresh chives
- Sriracha Mayo
- ½ cup mayonnaise
- 1 to 2 tablespoons sriracha hot sauce
- 1 tablespoon milk

Directions:

1. Cut the tomatoes in ¼-inch slices. Pat them dry with a clean kitchen towel and season generously with salt and pepper.
2. Set up a dredging station using three shallow dishes. Place the flour in the first shallow dish, whisk the eggs and buttermilk together in the second dish, and combine the panko breadcrumbs and cornmeal in the third dish.
3. Preheat the air fryer to 400°F.
4. Dredge the tomato slices in flour to coat on all sides. Then dip them into the egg mixture and finally press them into the breadcrumbs to coat all sides of the tomato.
5. Spray or brush the air-fryer basket with olive oil. Transfer 3 to 4 tomato slices into the basket and spray the top with olive oil. Air-fry the tomatoes at 400°F for 8 minutes. Flip them over,

spray the other side with oil and air-fry for an additional 4 minutes until golden brown.

6. While the tomatoes are cooking, make the sriracha mayo. Combine the mayonnaise, 1 tablespoon of the sriracha hot sauce and milk in a small bowl. Stir well until the mixture is smooth. Add more sriracha sauce to taste.

7. When the tomatoes are done, transfer them to a cooling rack or a platter lined with paper towels so the bottom does not get soggy. Before serving, carefully stack the all the tomatoes into air fryer and air-fry at 350°F for 1 to 2 minutes to heat them back up.

8. Serve the fried green tomatoes hot with the sriracha mayo on the side. Season one last time with salt and freshly ground black pepper and garnish with sprigs of fresh thyme or chopped fresh chives.

Brussels Sprout And Ham Salad

Servings: 3
Cooking Time: 12 Minutes

Ingredients:

- 1 pound 2-inch-in-length Brussels sprouts, quartered through the stem
- 6 ounces Smoked ham steak, any rind removed, diced (gluten-free, if a concern)
- ¼ teaspoon Caraway seeds
- Vegetable oil spray
- ¼ cup Brine from a jar of pickles (gluten-free, if a concern)
- ¾ teaspoon Ground black pepper

Directions:

1. Preheat the air fryer to 375°F .
2. Toss the Brussels sprout quarters, ham, and caraway seeds in a bowl until well combined. Generously coat the top of the mixture with vegetable oil spray, toss again, spray again, and repeat a couple of times until the vegetables and ham are glistening.

3. When the machine is at temperature, scrape the contents of the bowl into the basket, spreading it into as close to one layer as you can. Air-fry for 12 minutes, tossing and rearranging the pieces at least twice so that any covered or touching parts are eventually exposed to the air currents, until the Brussels sprouts are tender and a little brown at the edges.

4. Dump the contents of the basket into a serving bowl. Scrape any caraway seeds from the bottom of the basket or the tray under the basket attachment into the bowl as well. Add the pickle brine and pepper. Toss well to coat. Serve warm.

Fried Okra

Servings: 4
Cooking Time: 8 Minutes

Ingredients:

- 1 pound okra
- 1 large egg
- 1 tablespoon milk
- 1 teaspoon salt, divided
- ½ teaspoon black pepper, divided
- ¼ teaspoon paprika
- ¼ teaspoon thyme
- ½ cup cornmeal
- ½ cup all-purpose flour

Directions:

1. Preheat the air fryer to 400°F.
2. Cut the okra into ½-inch rounds.
3. In a medium bowl, whisk together the egg, milk, ½ teaspoon of the salt, and ¼ teaspoon of black pepper. Place the okra into the egg mixture and toss until well coated.

4. In a separate bowl, mix together the remaining ½ teaspoon of salt, the remaining ¼ teaspoon of black pepper, the paprika, the thyme, the cornmeal, and the flour. Working in small batches, dredge the egg-coated okra in the cornmeal mixture until all the okra has been breaded.

5. Place a single layer of okra in the air fryer basket and spray with cooking spray. Cook for 4 minutes, toss to check for crispness, and cook another 4 minutes. Repeat in batches, as needed.

Cheesy Potato Pot

Servings: 4
Cooking Time: 13 Minutes

Ingredients:

* 3 cups cubed red potatoes (unpeeled, cut into ½-inch cubes)
* ½ teaspoon garlic powder
* salt and pepper
* 1 tablespoon oil
* chopped chives for garnish (optional)
* Sauce
* 2 tablespoons milk
* 1 tablespoon butter
* 2 ounces sharp Cheddar cheese, grated
* 1 tablespoon sour cream

Directions:

1. Place potato cubes in large bowl and sprinkle with garlic, salt, and pepper. Add oil and stir to coat well.

2. Cook at 390°F for 13 minutes or until potatoes are tender. Stir every 4 or 5minutes during cooking time.

3. While potatoes are cooking, combine milk and butter in a small saucepan. Warm over medium-low heat to melt butter. Add cheese and stir until it melts. The melted cheese will remain separated from the milk mixture. Remove from heat until potatoes are done.

4. When ready to serve, add sour cream to cheese mixture and stir over medium-low heat just until warmed. Place cooked potatoes in serving bowl. Pour sauce over potatoes and stir to combine.

5. Garnish with chives if desired.

Crispy Cauliflower Puffs

Servings: 12
Cooking Time: 9 Minutes

Ingredients:

* 1½ cups Riced cauliflower
* 1 cup (about 4 ounces) Shredded Monterey Jack cheese
* ¾ cup Seasoned Italian-style panko bread crumbs (gluten-free, if a concern)
* 2 tablespoons plus 1 teaspoon All-purpose flour or potato starch
* 2 tablespoons plus 1 teaspoon Vegetable oil
* 1 plus 1 large yolk Large egg(s)
* ¾ teaspoon Table salt
* Vegetable oil spray

Directions:

1. Preheat the air fryer to 375°F .

2. Stir the riced cauliflower, cheese, bread crumbs, flour or potato starch, oil, egg(s) and egg yolk (if necessary), and salt in a large bowl to make a thick batter.

3. Using 2 tablespoons of the batter, form a compact ball between your clean, dry palms. Set it aside and continue forming more balls: 7 more for a small batch, 11 more for a medium batch, or 15 more for a large batch.

4. Generously coat the balls on all sides with vegetable oil spray. Set them in the basket with as much air space between them as possible. Air-fry undisturbed for 7 minutes, or until golden brown and crisp. If the machine is at 360°F, you may need to add 2 minutes to the cooking time.

5. Gently pour the contents of the basket onto a wire rack. Cool the puffs for 5 minutes before serving.

Glazed Carrots

Servings: 4
Cooking Time: 10 Minutes

Ingredients:
- 2 teaspoons honey
- 1 teaspoon orange juice
- ½ teaspoon grated orange rind
- ⅛ teaspoon ginger
- 1 pound baby carrots
- 2 teaspoons olive oil
- ¼ teaspoon salt

Directions:
1. Combine honey, orange juice, grated rind, and ginger in a small bowl and set aside.
2. Toss the carrots, oil, and salt together to coat well and pour them into the air fryer basket.
3. Cook at 390°F for 5minutes. Shake basket to stir a little and cook for 4 minutes more, until carrots are barely tender.
4. Pour carrots into air fryer baking pan.
5. Stir the honey mixture to combine well, pour glaze over carrots, and stir to coat.
6. Cook at 360°F for 1 minute or just until heated through.

Asparagus Fries

Servings: 4

Cooking Time: 5 Minutes Per Batch

Ingredients:
- 12 ounces fresh asparagus spears with tough ends trimmed off
- 2 egg whites
- ¼ cup water
- ¾ cup panko breadcrumbs
- ¼ cup grated Parmesan cheese, plus 2 tablespoons
- ¼ teaspoon salt
- oil for misting or cooking spray

Directions:
1. Preheat air fryer to 390°F.
2. In a shallow dish, beat egg whites and water until slightly foamy.
3. In another shallow dish, combine panko, Parmesan, and salt.
4. Dip asparagus spears in egg, then roll in crumbs. Spray with oil or cooking spray.
5. Place a layer of asparagus in air fryer basket, leaving just a little space in between each spear. Stack another layer on top, crosswise. Cook at 390°F for 5 minutes, until crispy and golden brown.
6. Repeat to cook remaining asparagus.

Mashed Potato Tots

Servings: 18
Cooking Time: 10 Minutes

Ingredients:
- 1 medium potato or 1 cup cooked mashed potatoes
- 1 tablespoon real bacon bits
- 2 tablespoons chopped green onions, tops only
- ¼ teaspoon onion powder
- 1 teaspoon dried chopped chives

- salt
- 2 tablespoons flour
- 1 egg white, beaten
- ½ cup panko breadcrumbs
- oil for misting or cooking spray

Directions:

1. If using cooked mashed potatoes, jump to step 4.

2. Peel potato and cut into ½-inch cubes. (Small pieces cook more quickly.) Place in saucepan, add water to cover, and heat to boil. Lower heat slightly and continue cooking just until tender, about 10minutes.

3. Drain potatoes and place in ice cold water. Allow to cool for a minute or two, then drain well and mash.

4. Preheat air fryer to 390°F.

5. In a large bowl, mix together the potatoes, bacon bits, onions, onion powder, chives, salt to taste, and flour. Add egg white and stir well.

6. Place panko crumbs on a sheet of wax paper.

7. For each tot, use about 2 teaspoons of potato mixture. To shape, drop the measure of potato mixture onto panko crumbs and push crumbs up and around potatoes to coat edges. Then turn tot over to coat other side with crumbs.

8. Mist tots with oil or cooking spray and place in air fryer basket, crowded but not stacked.

9. Cook at 390°F for 10 minutes, until browned and crispy.

10. Repeat steps 8 and 9 to cook remaining tots.

Perfect French Fries

Servings: 3
Cooking Time: 37 Minutes

Ingredients:

- 1 pound Large russet potato(es)
- Vegetable oil or olive oil spray
- ½ teaspoon Table salt

Directions:

1. Cut each potato lengthwise into ¼-inch-thick slices. Cut each of these lengthwise into ¼-inch-thick matchsticks.

2. Set the potato matchsticks in a big bowl of cool water and soak for 5 minutes. Drain in a colander set in the sink, then spread the matchsticks out on paper towels and dry them very well.

3. Preheat the air fryer to 225°F (or 230°F, if that's the closest setting).

4. When the machine is at temperature, arrange the matchsticks in an even layer (if overlapping but not compact) in the basket. Air-fry for 20 minutes, tossing and rearranging the fries twice.

5. Pour the contents of the basket into a big bowl. Increase the air fryer's temperature to 325°F (or 330°F, if that's the closest setting).

6. Generously coat the fries with vegetable or olive oil spray. Toss well, then coat them again to make sure they're covered on all sides, tossing (and maybe spraying) a couple of times to make sure.

7. When the machine is at temperature, pour the fries into the basket and air-fry for 12 minutes, tossing and rearranging the fries at least twice.

8. Increase the machine's temperature to 375°F (or 380°F or 390°F, if one of these is the closest setting). Air-fry for 5 minutes more (from the moment you raise the temperature), tossing and rearranging the fries at least twice to keep them from burning and to make sure they all get an even measure of the heat, until brown and crisp.

9. Pour the contents of the basket into a serving bowl. Toss the fries with the salt and serve hot.

Bacon-wrapped Asparagus

Servings: 4

Cooking Time: 10 Minutes

Ingredients:

- 1 tablespoon extra-virgin olive oil
- ½ teaspoon sea salt
- ¼ cup grated Parmesan cheese
- 1 pound asparagus, ends trimmed
- 8 slices bacon

Directions:

1. Preheat the air fryer to 380°F.

2. In large bowl, mix together the olive oil, sea salt, and Parmesan cheese. Toss the asparagus in the olive oil mixture.

3. Evenly divide the asparagus into 8 bundles. Wrap 1 piece of bacon around each bundle, not overlapping the bacon but spreading it across the bundle.

4. Place the asparagus bundles into the air fryer basket, not touching. Work in batches as needed.

5. Cook for 8 minutes; check for doneness, and cook another 2 minutes.

BREAD AND BREAKFAST

Roasted Vegetable Frittata

Servings: 1
Cooking Time: 19 Minutes

Ingredients:

- ½ red or green bell pepper, cut into ½-inch chunks
- 4 button mushrooms, sliced
- ½ cup diced zucchini
- ½ teaspoon chopped fresh oregano or thyme
- 1 teaspoon olive oil
- 3 eggs, beaten
- ½ cup grated Cheddar cheese
- salt and freshly ground black pepper, to taste
- 1 teaspoon butter
- 1 teaspoon chopped fresh parsley

Directions:

1. Preheat the air fryer to 400°F.
2. Toss the peppers, mushrooms, zucchini and oregano with the olive oil and air-fry for 6 minutes, shaking the basket once or twice during the cooking process to redistribute the ingredients.
3. While the vegetables are cooking, beat the eggs well in a bowl, stir in the Cheddar cheese and season with salt and freshly ground black pepper. Add the air-fried vegetables to this bowl when they have finished cooking.
4. Place a 6- or 7-inch non-stick metal cake pan into the air fryer basket with the butter using an aluminum sling to lower the pan into the basket. (Fold a piece of aluminum foil into a strip about 2-inches wide by 24-inches long.) Air-fry for 1 minute at 380°F to melt the butter. Remove the cake pan and rotate the pan to distribute the butter and grease the pan. Pour the egg mixture into the cake pan and return the pan to the air fryer, using the aluminum sling.
5. Air-fry at 380°F for 12 minutes, or until the frittata has puffed up and is lightly browned. Let the frittata sit in the air fryer for 5 minutes to cool to an edible temperature and set up. Remove the cake pan from the air fryer, sprinkle with parsley and serve immediately.

Mini Pita Breads

Servings: 8
Cooking Time: 6 Minutes

Ingredients:

- 2 teaspoons active dry yeast
- 1 tablespoon sugar
- 1¼ to 1½ cups warm water (90° - 110°F)
- 3¼ cups all-purpose flour
- 2 teaspoons salt
- 1 tablespoon olive oil, plus more for brushing
- kosher salt (optional)

Directions:

1. Dissolve the yeast, sugar and water in the bowl of a stand mixer. Let the mixture sit for 5 minutes to make sure the yeast is active – it should foam a little. (If there's no foaming, discard and start again with new yeast.) Combine the flour and salt in a bowl, and add it to the water, along with the olive oil. Mix with the dough hook until combined. Add a little more flour if needed to get the dough to pull away from the sides of the mixing bowl, or add a little more water if the dough seems too dry.
2. Knead the dough until it is smooth and elastic (about 8 minutes in the mixer or 15 minutes by hand). Transfer the dough to a lightly oiled bowl,

cover and let it rise in a warm place until doubled in bulk. Divide the dough into 8 portions and roll each portion into a circle about 4-inches in diameter. Don't roll the balls too thin, or you won't get the pocket inside the pita.

3. Preheat the air fryer to 400°F.

4. Brush both sides of the dough with olive oil, and sprinkle with kosher salt if desired. Air-fry one at a time at 400°F for 6 minutes, flipping it over when there are two minutes left in the cooking time.

Western Omelet

Servings: 2

Cooking Time: 22 Minutes

Ingredients:

- ¼ cup chopped onion
- ¼ cup chopped bell pepper, green or red
- ¼ cup diced ham
- 1 teaspoon butter
- 4 large eggs
- 2 tablespoons milk
- ⅛ teaspoon salt
- ¾ cup grated sharp Cheddar cheese

Directions:

1. Place onion, bell pepper, ham, and butter in air fryer baking pan. Cook at 390°F for 1 minute and stir. Continue cooking 5minutes, until vegetables are tender.

2. Beat together eggs, milk, and salt. Pour over vegetables and ham in baking pan. Cook at 360°F for 15minutes or until eggs set and top has browned slightly.

3. Sprinkle grated cheese on top of omelet. Cook 1 minute or just long enough to melt the cheese.

Garlic-cheese Biscuits

Servings: 8

Cooking Time: 8 Minutes

Ingredients:

- 1 cup self-rising flour
- 1 teaspoon garlic powder
- 2 tablespoons butter, diced
- 2 ounces sharp Cheddar cheese, grated
- ½ cup milk
- cooking spray

Directions:

1. Preheat air fryer to 330°F.

2. Combine flour and garlic in a medium bowl and stir together.

3. Using a pastry blender or knives, cut butter into dry ingredients.

4. Stir in cheese.

5. Add milk and stir until stiff dough forms.

6. If dough is too sticky to handle, stir in 1 or 2 more tablespoons of self-rising flour before shaping. Biscuits should be firm enough to hold their shape. Otherwise, they'll stick to the air fryer basket.

7. Divide dough into 8 portions and shape into 2-inch biscuits about ¾-inch thick.

8. Spray air fryer basket with nonstick cooking spray.

9. Place all 8 biscuits in basket and cook at 330°F for 8 minutes.

Carrot Orange Muffins

Servings: 12

Cooking Time: 12 Minutes

Ingredients:

- 1½ cups all-purpose flour
- ½ cup granulated sugar
- ½ teaspoon ground cinnamon
- 2 teaspoons baking powder
- ¼ teaspoon baking soda
- ½ teaspoon salt
- 2 large eggs
- ¼ cup vegetable oil
- ⅓ cup orange marmalade
- 2 cups grated carrots

Directions:

1. Preheat the air fryer to 320°F.

2. In a large bowl, whisk together the flour, sugar, cinnamon, baking powder, baking soda, and salt; set aside.

3. In a separate bowl, whisk together the eggs, vegetable oil, orange marmalade, and grated carrots.

4. Make a well in the dry ingredients; then pour the wet ingredients into the well of the dry ingredients. Using a rubber spatula, mix the ingredients for 1 minute or until slightly lumpy.

5. Using silicone muffin liners, fill 6 muffin liners two-thirds full.

6. Carefully place the muffin liners in the air fryer basket and bake for 12 minutes (or until the tops are browned and a toothpick inserted in the center comes out clean). Carefully remove the muffins from the basket and repeat with remaining batter.

7. Serve warm.

Hashbrown Potatoes Lyonnaise

Servings: 4

Cooking Time: 33 Minutes

Ingredients:

- 1 Vidalia (or other sweet) onion, sliced
- 1 teaspoon butter, melted
- 1 teaspoon brown sugar
- 2 large russet potatoes (about 1 pound), sliced ½-inch thick
- 1 tablespoon vegetable oil
- salt and freshly ground black pepper

Directions:

1. Preheat the air fryer to 370°F.

2. Toss the sliced onions, melted butter and brown sugar together in the air fryer basket. Air-fry for 8 minutes, shaking the basket occasionally to help the onions cook evenly.

3. While the onions are cooking, bring a 3-quart saucepan of salted water to a boil on the stovetop. Par-cook the potatoes in boiling water for 3 minutes. Drain the potatoes and pat them dry with a clean kitchen towel.

4. Add the potatoes to the onions in the air fryer basket and drizzle with vegetable oil. Toss to coat the potatoes with the oil and season with salt and freshly ground black pepper.

5. Increase the air fryer temperature to 400°F and air-fry for 22 minutes tossing the vegetables a few times during the cooking time to help the potatoes brown evenly. Season to taste again with salt and freshly ground black pepper and serve warm.

Hush Puffins

Servings: 20
Cooking Time: 8 Minutes

Ingredients:
- 1 cup buttermilk
- ¼ cup butter, melted
- 2 eggs
- 1½ cups all-purpose flour
- 1½ cups cornmeal
- ⅓ cup sugar
- 1 teaspoon baking soda
- 1 teaspoon salt
- 4 scallions, minced
- vegetable oil

Directions:

1. Combine the buttermilk, butter and eggs in a large mixing bowl. In a second bowl combine the flour, cornmeal, sugar, baking soda and salt. Add the dry ingredients to the wet ingredients, stirring just to combine. Stir in the minced scallions and refrigerate the batter for 30 minutes.

2. Shape the batter into 2-inch balls. Brush or spray the balls with oil.

3. Preheat the air fryer to 360°F.

4. Air-fry the hush puffins in two batches at 360°F for 8 minutes, turning them over after 6 minutes of the cooking process.

5. Serve warm with butter.

Southern Sweet Cornbread

Servings: 6
Cooking Time: 17 Minutes

Ingredients:
- cooking spray
- ½ cup white cornmeal
- ½ cup flour
- 2 teaspoons baking powder
- ½ teaspoon salt
- 4 teaspoons sugar
- 1 egg
- 2 tablespoons oil
- ½ cup milk

Directions:

1. Preheat air fryer to 360°F.

2. Spray air fryer baking pan with nonstick cooking spray.

3. In a medium bowl, stir together the cornmeal, flour, baking powder, salt, and sugar.

4. In a small bowl, beat together the egg, oil, and milk. Stir into dry ingredients until well combined.

5. Pour batter into prepared baking pan.

6. Cook at 360°F for 17 minutes or until toothpick inserted in center comes out clean or with crumbs clinging.

Baked Eggs

Servings: 4
Cooking Time: 6 Minutes

Ingredients:
- 4 large eggs
- ⅛ teaspoon black pepper
- ⅛ teaspoon salt

Directions:

1. Preheat the air fryer to 330°F. Place 4 silicone muffin liners into the air fryer basket.

2. Crack 1 egg at a time into each silicone muffin liner. Sprinkle with black pepper and salt.

3. Bake for 6 minutes. Remove and let cool 2 minutes prior to serving.

Classic Cinnamon Rolls

Servings: 4

Cooking Time: 6 Minutes

Ingredients:

- 1½ cups all-purpose flour
- 1 tablespoon granulated sugar
- 2 teaspoons baking powder
- ½ teaspoon salt
- 4 tablespoons butter, divided
- ½ cup buttermilk
- 2 tablespoons brown sugar
- 1 teaspoon cinnamon
- 1 cup powdered sugar
- 2 tablespoons milk

Directions:

1. Preheat the air fryer to 360°F.

2. In a large bowl, stir together the flour, sugar, baking powder, and salt. Cut in 3 tablespoons of the butter with a pastry blender or two knives until coarse crumbs remain. Stir in the buttermilk until a dough forms.

3. Place the dough onto a floured surface and roll out into a square shape about ½ inch thick.

4. Melt the remaining 1 tablespoon of butter in the microwave for 20 seconds. Using a pastry brush or your fingers, spread the melted butter onto the dough.

5. In a small bowl, mix together the brown sugar and cinnamon. Sprinkle the mixture across the surface of the dough. Roll the dough up, forming a long log. Using a pastry cutter or sharp knife, cut 10 cinnamon rolls.

6. Carefully place the cinnamon rolls into the air fryer basket. Then bake at 360°F for 6 minutes or until golden brown.

7. Meanwhile, in a small bowl, whisk together the powdered sugar and milk.

8. Plate the cinnamon rolls and drizzle the glaze over the surface before serving.

Mini Everything Bagels

Servings: 4

Cooking Time: 6 Minutes

Ingredients:

- 1 cup all-purpose flour
- 2 teaspoons baking powder
- ½ teaspoon salt
- 1 cup plain Greek yogurt
- 1 egg, whisked
- 1 teaspoon sesame seeds
- 1 teaspoon dehydrated onions
- ½ teaspoon poppy seeds
- ½ teaspoon garlic powder
- ½ teaspoon sea salt flakes

Directions:

1. In a large bowl, mix together the flour, baking powder, and salt. Make a well in the dough and add in the Greek yogurt. Mix with a spoon until a dough forms.

2. Place the dough onto a heavily floured surface and knead for 3 minutes. You may use up to 1 cup of additional flour as you knead the dough, if necessary.

3. Cut the dough into 8 pieces and roll each piece into a 6-inch, snakelike piece. Touch the ends of each piece together so it closes the circle and forms a bagel shape. Brush the tops of the bagels with the whisked egg.

4. In a small bowl, combine the sesame seeds, dehydrated onions, poppy seeds, garlic powder, and sea salt flakes. Sprinkle the seasoning on top of the bagels.

5. Preheat the air fryer to 360°F. Using a bench scraper or flat-edged spatula, carefully place the

bagels into the air fryer basket. Spray the bagel tops with cooking spray. Air-fry the bagels for 6 minutes or until golden brown. Allow the bread to cool at least 10 minutes before slicing for serving.

Strawberry Streusel Muffins

Servings: 12

Cooking Time: 14 Minutes

Ingredients:

- 1¾ cups all-purpose flour
- ½ cup granulated sugar
- 2 teaspoons baking powder
- ¼ teaspoon baking soda
- ½ teaspoon salt
- ½ cup plain yogurt
- ½ cup milk
- ¼ cup vegetable oil
- 2 large eggs
- 1 teaspoon vanilla extract
- ½ cup freeze-dried strawberries
- 2 tablespoons brown sugar
- ¼ cup oats
- 2 tablespoons butter

Directions:

1. Preheat the air fryer to 330°F.
2. In a large bowl, whisk together the flour, sugar, baking powder, baking soda, and salt; set aside.
3. In a separate bowl, whisk together the yogurt, milk, vegetable oil, eggs, and vanilla extract.
4. Make a well in the dry ingredients; then pour the wet ingredients into the well of the dry ingredients. Using a rubber spatula, mix the ingredients for 1 minute or until slightly lumpy. Fold in the strawberries.

5. In a small bowl, use your fingers to mix together the brown sugar, oats, and butter until coarse crumbles appear. Divide the mixture in half.
6. Using silicone muffin liners, fill 6 muffin liners two-thirds full.
7. Crumble half of the streusel topping onto the first batch of muffins.
8. Carefully place the muffin liners in the air fryer basket and bake for 14 minutes (or until the tops are browned and a toothpick inserted in the center comes out clean). Carefully remove the muffins from the basket and repeat with the remaining batter and topping.
9. Serve warm.

Cajun Breakfast Potatoes

Servings: 4

Cooking Time: 20 Minutes

Ingredients:

- 1 pound roasting potatoes (like russet), scrubbed clean
- 1 tablespoon vegetable oil
- 2 teaspoons paprika
- ½ teaspoon garlic powder
- ¼ teaspoon onion powder
- ¼ teaspoon ground cumin
- 1 teaspoon thyme
- 1 teaspoon sea salt
- ½ teaspoon black pepper

Directions:

1. Cut the potatoes into 1-inch cubes.
2. In a large bowl, toss the cut potatoes with vegetable oil.
3. Sprinkle paprika, garlic powder, onion powder, cumin, thyme, salt, and pepper onto the potatoes, and toss to coat well.

4.   Preheat the air fryer to 400°F for 4 minutes.

5.   Add the potatoes to the air fryer basket and bake for 10 minutes. Stir or toss the potatoes and continue baking for an additional 5 minutes. Stir or toss again and continue baking for an additional 5 minutes or until the desired crispness is achieved.

Cinnamon Sugar Donut Holes

Servings: 12

Cooking Time: 6 Minutes

Ingredients:

- 1 cup all-purpose flour
- 6 tablespoons cane sugar, divided
- 1 teaspoon baking powder
- 3 teaspoons ground cinnamon, divided
- ¼ teaspoon salt
- 1 large egg
- 1 teaspoon vanilla extract
- 2 tablespoons melted butter

Directions:

1.   Preheat the air fryer to 370°F.

2.   In a small bowl, combine the flour, 2 tablespoons of the sugar, the baking powder, 1 teaspoon of the cinnamon, and the salt. Mix well.

3.   In a larger bowl, whisk together the egg, vanilla extract, and butter.

4.   Slowly add the dry ingredients into the wet until all the ingredients are uniformly combined. Set the bowl inside the refrigerator for at least 30 minutes.

5.   Before you're ready to cook, in a small bowl, mix together the remaining 4 tablespoons of sugar and 2 teaspoons of cinnamon.

6.   Liberally spray the air fryer basket with olive oil mist so the donut holes don't stick to the bottom. Note: You do not want to use parchment paper in this recipe; it may burn if your air fryer is hotter than others.

7.   Remove the dough from the refrigerator and divide it into 12 equal donut holes. You can use a 1-ounce serving scoop if you have one.

8.   Roll each donut hole in the sugar and cinnamon mixture; then place in the air fryer basket. Repeat until all the donut holes are covered in the sugar and cinnamon mixture.

9.   When the basket is full, cook for 6 minutes. Remove the donut holes from the basket using oven-safe tongs and let cool 5 minutes. Repeat until all 12 are cooked.

Roasted Tomato And Cheddar Rolls

Servings: 12

Cooking Time: 55 Minutes

Ingredients:

- 4 Roma tomatoes
- ½ clove garlic, minced
- 1 tablespoon olive oil
- ¼ teaspoon dried thyme
- salt and freshly ground black pepper
- 4 cups all-purpose flour
- 1 teaspoon active dry yeast
- 2 teaspoons sugar
- 2 teaspoons salt
- 1 tablespoon olive oil
- 1 cup grated Cheddar cheese, plus more for sprinkling at the end
- 1½ cups water

Directions:

1.   Cut the Roma tomatoes in half, remove the seeds with your fingers and transfer to a bowl. Add the garlic, olive oil, dried thyme, salt and freshly ground black pepper and toss well.

2. Preheat the air fryer to 390°F.

3. Place the tomatoes, cut side up in the air fryer basket and air-fry for 10 minutes. The tomatoes should just start to brown. Shake the basket to redistribute the tomatoes, and air-fry for another 5 to 10 minutes at 330°F until the tomatoes are no longer juicy. Let the tomatoes cool and then rough chop them.

4. Combine the flour, yeast, sugar and salt in the bowl of a stand mixer. Add the olive oil, chopped roasted tomatoes and Cheddar cheese to the flour mixture and start to mix using the dough hook attachment. As you're mixing, add 1¼ cups of the water, mixing until the dough comes together. Continue to knead the dough with the dough hook for another 10 minutes, adding enough water to the dough to get it to the right consistency.

5. Transfer the dough to an oiled bowl, cover with a clean kitchen towel and let it rest and rise until it has doubled in volume – about 1 to 2 hours. Then, divide the dough into 12 equal portions. Roll each portion of dough into a ball. Lightly coat each dough ball with oil and let the dough balls rest and rise a second time, covered lightly with plastic wrap for 45 minutes. (Alternately, you can place the rolls in the refrigerator overnight and take them out 2 hours before you bake them.)

6. Preheat the air fryer to 360°F.

7. Spray the dough balls and the air fryer basket with a little olive oil. Place three rolls at a time in the basket and bake for 10 minutes. Add a little grated Cheddar cheese on top of the rolls for the last 2 minutes of air frying for an attractive finish.

Crustless Broccoli, Roasted Pepper And Fontina Quiche

Servings: 4
Cooking Time: 60 Minutes

Ingredients:
- 7-inch cake pan
- 1 cup broccoli florets
- ¾ cup chopped roasted red peppers
- 1¼ cups grated Fontina cheese
- 6 eggs
- ¾ cup heavy cream
- ½ teaspoon salt
- freshly ground black pepper

Directions:
1. Preheat the air fryer to 360°F.

2. Grease the inside of a 7-inch cake pan (4 inches deep) or other oven-safe pan that will fit into your air fryer. Place the broccoli florets and roasted red peppers in the cake pan and top with the grated Fontina cheese.

3. Whisk the eggs and heavy cream together in a bowl. Season the eggs with salt and freshly ground black pepper. Pour the egg mixture over the cheese and vegetables and cover the pan with aluminum foil. Transfer the cake pan to the air fryer basket.

4. Air-fry at 360°F for 60 minutes. Remove the aluminum foil for the last two minutes of cooking time.

5. Unmold the quiche onto a platter and cut it into slices to serve with a side salad or perhaps some air-fried potatoes.

Cinnamon Rolls With Cream Cheese Glaze

Servings: 8
Cooking Time: 9 Minutes

Ingredients:
- 1 pound frozen bread dough, thawed
- ¼ cup butter, melted and cooled
- ¾ cup brown sugar
- 1½ tablespoons ground cinnamon
- Cream Cheese Glaze:
- 4 ounces cream cheese, softened
- 2 tablespoons butter, softened
- 1¼ cups powdered sugar
- ½ teaspoon vanilla

Directions:
1. Let the bread dough come to room temperature on the counter. On a lightly floured surface roll the dough into a 13-inch by 11-inch rectangle. Position the rectangle so the 13-inch side is facing you. Brush the melted butter all over the dough, leaving a 1-inch border uncovered along the edge farthest away from you.

2. Combine the brown sugar and cinnamon in a small bowl. Sprinkle the mixture evenly over the buttered dough, keeping the 1-inch border uncovered. Roll the dough into a log starting with the edge closest to you. Roll the dough tightly, making sure to roll evenly and push out any air pockets. When you get to the uncovered edge of the dough, press the dough onto the roll to seal it together.

3. Cut the log into 8 pieces slicing slowly with a sawing motion so you don't flatten the dough. Turn the slices on their sides and cover with a clean kitchen towel. Let the rolls sit in the warmest part of your kitchen for 1½ to 2 hours to rise.

4. To make the glaze, place the cream cheese and butter in a microwave-safe bowl. Soften the mixture in the microwave for 30 seconds at a time until it is easy to stir. Gradually add the powdered sugar and stir to combine. Add the vanilla extract and whisk until smooth. Set aside.

5. When the rolls have risen, Preheat the air fryer to 350°F.

6. Transfer 4 of the rolls to the air fryer basket. Air-fry for 5 minutes. Turn the rolls over and air-fry for another 4 minutes. Repeat with the remaining 4 rolls.

7. Let the rolls cool for a couple of minutes before glazing. Spread large dollops of cream cheese glaze on top of the warm cinnamon rolls, allowing some of the glaze to drip down the side of the rolls. Serve warm and enjoy!

Mediterranean Egg Sandwich

Servings: 1
Cooking Time: 8 Minutes

Ingredients:
- 1 large egg
- 5 baby spinach leaves, chopped
- 1 tablespoon roasted bell pepper, chopped
- 1 English muffin
- 1 thin slice prosciutto or Canadian bacon

Directions:
1. Spray a ramekin with cooking spray or brush the inside with extra-virgin olive oil.

2. In a small bowl, whisk together the egg, baby spinach, and bell pepper.

3. Split the English muffin in half and spray the inside lightly with cooking spray or brush with extra-virgin olive oil.

4. Preheat the air fryer to 350°F for 2 minutes. Place the egg ramekin and open English muffin into the air fryer basket, and cook at 350°F for 5 minutes. Open the air fryer drawer and add the prosciutto or bacon; cook for an additional 1 minute.

5. To assemble the sandwich, place the egg on one half of the English muffin, top with prosciutto or bacon, and place the remaining piece of English muffin on top.

Pumpkin Loaf

Servings: 6
Cooking Time: 22 Minutes

Ingredients:
- cooking spray
- 1 large egg
- ½ cup granulated sugar
- ⅓ cup oil
- ½ cup canned pumpkin (not pie filling)
- ½ teaspoon vanilla
- ⅔ cup flour plus 1 tablespoon
- ½ teaspoon baking powder
- ½ teaspoon baking soda
- ½ teaspoon salt
- 1 teaspoon pumpkin pie spice
- ¼ teaspoon cinnamon

Directions:
1. Spray 6 x 6-inch baking dish lightly with cooking spray.
2. Place baking dish in air fryer basket and preheat air fryer to 330°F.
3. In a large bowl, beat eggs and sugar together with a hand mixer.
4. Add oil, pumpkin, and vanilla and mix well.
5. Sift together all dry ingredients. Add to pumpkin mixture and beat well, about 1 minute.
6. Pour batter in baking dish and cook at 330°F for 22 minutes or until toothpick inserted in center of loaf comes out clean.

Broccoli Cornbread

Servings: 6
Cooking Time: 18 Minutes

Ingredients:
- 1 cup frozen chopped broccoli, thawed and drained
- ¼ cup cottage cheese
- 1 egg, beaten
- 2 tablespoons minced onion
- 2 tablespoons melted butter
- ½ cup flour
- ½ cup yellow cornmeal
- 1 teaspoon baking powder
- ½ teaspoon salt
- ¼ cup milk, plus 2 tablespoons
- cooking spray

Directions:
1. Place thawed broccoli in colander and press with a spoon to squeeze out excess moisture.
2. Stir together all ingredients in a large bowl.
3. Spray 6 x 6-inch baking pan with cooking spray.
4. Spread batter in pan and cook at 330°F for 18 minutes or until cornbread is lightly browned and loaf starts to pull away from sides of pan.

Garlic Bread Knots

Servings: 8
Cooking Time: 5 Minutes

Ingredients:
- ¼ cup melted butter
- 2 teaspoons garlic powder
- 1 teaspoon dried parsley

- 1 (11-ounce) tube of refrigerated French bread dough

Directions:

1. Mix the melted butter, garlic powder and dried parsley in a small bowl and set it aside.

2. To make smaller knots, cut the long tube of bread dough into 16 slices. If you want to make bigger knots, slice the dough into 8 slices. Shape each slice into a long rope about 6 inches long by rolling it on a flat surface with the palm of your hands. Tie each rope into a knot and place them on a plate.

3. Preheat the air fryer to 350°F.

4. Transfer half of the bread knots into the air fryer basket, leaving space in between each knot. Brush each knot with the butter mixture using a pastry brush.

5. Air-fry for 5 minutes. Remove the baked knots and brush a little more of the garlic butter mixture on each. Repeat with the remaining bread knots and serve warm.

Chocolate Almond Crescent Rolls

Servings: 4
Cooking Time: 8 Minutes

Ingredients:

- 1 (8-ounce) tube of crescent roll dough
- ⅔ cup semi-sweet or bittersweet chocolate chunks
- 1 egg white, lightly beaten
- ¼ cup sliced almonds
- powdered sugar, for dusting
- butter or oil

Directions:

1. Preheat the air fryer to 350°F.

2. Unwrap the crescent roll dough and separate it into triangles with the points facing away from you. Place a row of chocolate chunks along the bottom edge of the dough. (If you are using chips, make it a double row.) Roll the dough up around the chocolate and then place another row of chunks on the dough. Roll again and finish with one or two chocolate chunks. Be sure to leave the end free of chocolate so that it can adhere to the rest of the roll.

3. Brush the tops of the crescent rolls with the lightly beaten egg white and sprinkle the almonds on top, pressing them into the crescent dough so they adhere.

4. Brush the bottom of the air fryer basket with butter or oil and transfer the crescent rolls to the basket. Air-fry at 350°F for 8 minutes. Remove and let the crescent rolls cool before dusting with powdered sugar and serving.

Peach Fritters

Servings: 8
Cooking Time: 6 Minutes

Ingredients:

- 1½ cups bread flour
- 1 teaspoon active dry yeast
- ¼ cup sugar
- ¼ teaspoon salt
- ½ cup warm milk
- ½ teaspoon vanilla extract
- 2 egg yolks
- 2 tablespoons melted butter
- 2 cups small diced peaches (fresh or frozen)
- 1 tablespoon butter
- 1 teaspoon ground cinnamon
- 1 to 2 tablespoons sugar
- Glaze
- ¾ cup powdered sugar
- 4 teaspoons milk

Directions:

1. Combine the flour, yeast, sugar and salt in a bowl. Add the milk, vanilla, egg yolks and melted butter and combine until the dough starts to come together. Transfer the dough to a floured surface and knead it by hand for 2 minutes. Shape the dough into a ball, place it in a large oiled bowl, cover with a clean kitchen towel and let the dough rise in a warm place for 1 to 1½ hours, or until the dough has doubled in size.

2. While the dough is rising, melt one tablespoon of butter in a medium saucepan on the stovetop. Add the diced peaches, cinnamon and sugar to taste. Cook the peaches for about 5 minutes, or until they soften. Set the peaches aside to cool.

3. When the dough has risen, transfer it to a floured surface and shape it into a 12-inch circle. Spread the peaches over half of the circle and fold the other half of the dough over the top. With a knife or a board scraper, score the dough by making slits in the dough in a diamond shape. Push the knife straight down into the dough and peaches, rather than slicing through. You should cut through the top layer of dough, but not the bottom. Roll the dough up into a log from one short end to the other. It should be roughly 8 inches long. Some of the peaches will be sticking out of the dough – don't worry, these are supposed to be a little random. Cut the log into 8 equal slices. Place the dough disks on a floured cookie sheet, cover with a clean kitchen towel and let rise in a warm place for 30 minutes.

4. Preheat the air fryer to 370°F.

5. Air-fry 2 or 3 fritters at a time at 370°F, for 3 minutes. Flip them over and continue to air-fry for another 2 to 3 minutes, until they are golden brown.

6. Combine the powdered sugar and milk together in a small bowl. Whisk vigorously until smooth. Allow the fritters to cool for at least 10 minutes and then brush the glaze over both the bottom and top of each one. Serve warm or at room temperature.

Goat Cheese, Beet, And Kale Frittata

Servings: 6
Cooking Time: 20 Minutes

Ingredients:

- 6 large eggs
- ½ teaspoon garlic powder
- ¼ teaspoon black pepper
- ¼ teaspoon salt
- 1 cup chopped kale
- 1 cup cooked and chopped red beets
- ⅓ cup crumbled goat cheese

Directions:

1. Preheat the air fryer to 320°F.

2. In a medium bowl, whisk the eggs with the garlic powder, pepper, and salt. Mix in the kale, beets, and goat cheese.

3. Spray an oven-safe 7-inch springform pan with cooking spray. Pour the egg mixture into the pan and place it in the air fryer basket.

4. Cook for 20 minutes, or until the internal temperature reaches 145°F.

5. When the frittata is cooked, let it set for 5 minutes before removing from the pan.

6. Slice and serve immediately.

Whole-grain Cornbread

Servings: 6

Cooking Time: 25 Minutes

Ingredients:

- 1 cup stoneground cornmeal
- ½ cup brown rice flour
- 1 teaspoon sugar
- 2 teaspoons baking powder
- ¼ teaspoon salt
- 1 cup milk
- 2 tablespoons oil
- 2 eggs
- cooking spray

Directions:

1. Preheat the air fryer to 360°F.

2. In a medium mixing bowl, mix cornmeal, brown rice flour, sugar, baking powder, and salt together.

3. Add the remaining ingredients and beat with a spoon until batter is smooth.

4. Spray air fryer baking pan with nonstick cooking spray and add the cornbread batter.

5. Bake at 360°F for 25 minutes, until center is done.

DESSERTS AND SWEETS

Grilled Pineapple Dessert

Servings: 4
Cooking Time: 12 Minutes

Ingredients:
- oil for misting or cooking spray
- 4 ½-inch-thick slices fresh pineapple, core removed
- 1 tablespoon honey
- ¼ teaspoon brandy
- 2 tablespoons slivered almonds, toasted
- vanilla frozen yogurt or coconut sorbet

Directions:
1. Spray both sides of pineapple slices with oil or cooking spray. Place on grill plate or directly into air fryer basket.
2. Cook at 390°F for 6minutes. Turn slices over and cook for an additional 6minutes.
3. Mix together the honey and brandy.
4. Remove cooked pineapple slices from air fryer, sprinkle with toasted almonds, and drizzle with honey mixture.
5. Serve with a scoop of frozen yogurt or sorbet on the side.

Fried Pineapple Chunks

Servings: 3
Cooking Time: 10 Minutes

Ingredients:
- 3 tablespoons Cornstarch
- 1 Large egg white, beaten until foamy
- 1 cup (4 ounces) Ground vanilla wafer cookies (not low-fat cookies)
- ¼ teaspoon Ground dried ginger
- 18 (about 2¼ cups) Fresh 1-inch chunks peeled and cored pineapple

Directions:
1. Preheat the air fryer to 400°F.
2. Put the cornstarch in a medium or large bowl. Put the beaten egg white in a small bowl. Pour the cookie crumbs and ground dried ginger into a large zip-closed plastic bag, shaking it a bit to combine them.
3. Dump the pineapple chunks into the bowl with the cornstarch. Toss and stir until well coated. Use your cleaned fingers or a large fork like a shovel to pick up a few pineapple chunks, shake off any excess cornstarch, and put them in the bowl with the egg white. Stir gently, then pick them up and let any excess egg white slip back into the rest. Put them in the bag with the crumb mixture. Repeat the cornstarch-then-egg process until all the pineapple chunks are in the bag. Seal the bag and shake gently, turning the bag this way and that, to coat the pieces well.
4. Set the coated pineapple chunks in the basket with as much air space between them as possible. Even a fraction of an inch will work, but they should not touch. Air-fry undisturbed for 10 minutes, or until golden brown and crisp.
5. Gently dump the contents of the basket onto a wire rack. Cool for at least 5 minutes or up to 15 minutes before serving.

Coconut-custard Pie

Servings: 4

Cooking Time: 20 Minutes

Ingredients:

- 1 cup milk
- ¼ cup plus 2 tablespoons sugar
- ¼ cup biscuit baking mix
- 1 teaspoon vanilla
- 2 eggs
- 2 tablespoons melted butter
- cooking spray
- ½ cup shredded, sweetened coconut

Directions:

1. Place all ingredients except coconut in a medium bowl.

2. Using a hand mixer, beat on high speed for 3minutes.

3. Let sit for 5minutes.

4. Preheat air fryer to 330°F.

5. Spray a 6-inch round or 6 x 6-inch square baking pan with cooking spray and place pan in air fryer basket.

6. Pour filling into pan and sprinkle coconut over top.

7. Cook pie at 330°F for 20 minutes or until center sets.

Boston Cream Donut Holes

Servings: 24

Cooking Time: 12 Minutes

Ingredients:

- 1½ cups bread flour
- 1 teaspoon active dry yeast
- 1 tablespoon sugar
- ¼ teaspoon salt
- ½ cup warm milk
- ½ teaspoon pure vanilla extract
- 2 egg yolks
- 2 tablespoons butter, melted
- vegetable oil
- Custard Filling:
- 1 (3.4-ounce) box French vanilla instant pudding mix
- ¾ cup whole milk
- ¼ cup heavy cream
- Chocolate Glaze:
- 1 cup chocolate chips
- ⅓ cup heavy cream

Directions:

1. Combine the flour, yeast, sugar and salt in the bowl of a stand mixer. Add the milk, vanilla, egg yolks and butter. Mix until the dough starts to come together in a ball. Transfer the dough to a floured surface and knead the dough by hand for 2 minutes. Shape the dough into a ball, place it in a large oiled bowl, cover the bowl with a clean kitchen towel and let the dough rise for 1 to 1½ hours or until the dough has doubled in size.

2. When the dough has risen, punch it down and roll it into a 24-inch log. Cut the dough into 24 pieces and roll each piece into a ball. Place the dough balls on a baking sheet and let them rise for another 30 minutes.

3. Preheat the air fryer to 400°F.

4. Spray or brush the dough balls lightly with vegetable oil and air-fry eight at a time for 4 minutes, turning them over halfway through the cooking time.

5. While donut holes are cooking, make the filling and chocolate glaze. To make the filling, use an electric hand mixer to beat the French vanilla pudding, milk and ¼ cup of heavy cream together for 2 minutes.

6. To make the chocolate glaze, place the chocolate chips in a medium-sized bowl. Bring the heavy cream to a boil on the stovetop and pour it over the chocolate chips. Stir until the chips are melted and the glaze is smooth.

7. To fill the donut holes, place the custard filling in a pastry bag with a long tip. Poke a hole into the side of the donut hole with a small knife. Wiggle the knife around to make room for the filling. Place the pastry bag tip into the hole and slowly squeeze the custard into the center of the donut. Dip the top half of the donut into the chocolate glaze, letting any excess glaze drip back into the bowl. Let the glazed donut holes sit for a few minutes before serving.

Chocolate Cake

Servings: 8
Cooking Time: 20 Minutes

Ingredients:
- ½ cup sugar
- ¼ cup flour, plus 3 tablespoons
- 3 tablespoons cocoa
- ½ teaspoon baking powder
- ½ teaspoon baking soda
- ¼ teaspoon salt
- 1 egg
- 2 tablespoons oil
- ½ cup milk
- ½ teaspoon vanilla extract

Directions:
1. Preheat air fryer to 330°F.
2. Grease and flour a 6 x 6-inch baking pan.
3. In a medium bowl, stir together the sugar, flour, cocoa, baking powder, baking soda, and salt.
4. Add all other ingredients and beat with a wire whisk until smooth.

5. Pour batter into prepared pan and bake at 330°F for 20 minutes, until toothpick inserted in center comes out clean or with crumbs clinging to it.

Annie's Chocolate Chunk Hazelnut Cookies

Servings: 24
Cooking Time: 12 Minutes

Ingredients:
- 1 cup butter, softened
- 1 cup brown sugar
- ½ cup granulated sugar
- 2 eggs, lightly beaten
- 1½ teaspoons vanilla extract
- 1½ cups all-purpose flour
- ½ cup rolled oats
- 1 teaspoon baking soda
- ½ teaspoon salt
- 2 cups chocolate chunks
- ½ cup toasted chopped hazelnuts

Directions:
1. Cream the butter and sugars together until light and fluffy using a stand mixer or electric hand mixer. Add the eggs and vanilla, and beat until well combined.
2. Combine the flour, rolled oats, baking soda and salt in a second bowl. Gradually add the dry ingredients to the wet ingredients with a wooden spoon or spatula. Stir in the chocolate chunks and hazelnuts until distributed throughout the dough.
3. Shape the cookies into small balls about the size of golf balls and place them on a baking sheet. Freeze the cookie balls for at least 30 minutes, or package them in as airtight a package as you can and keep them in your freezer.

4. When you're ready for a delicious snack or dessert, Preheat the air fryer to 350°F. Cut a piece of parchment paper to fit the number of cookies you are baking. Place the parchment down in the air fryer basket and place the frozen cookie ball or balls on top (remember to leave room for them to expand).

5. Air-fry the cookies at 350°F for 12 minutes, or until they are done to your liking. Let them cool for a few minutes before enjoying your freshly baked cookie.

Midnight Nutella® Banana Sandwich

Servings: 2
Cooking Time: 8 Minutes

Ingredients:
- butter, softened
- 4 slices white bread*
- ¼ cup chocolate hazelnut spread (Nutella®)
- 1 banana

Directions:
1. Preheat the air fryer to 370°F.
2. Spread the softened butter on one side of all the slices of bread and place the slices buttered side down on the counter. Spread the chocolate hazelnut spread on the other side of the bread slices. Cut the banana in half and then slice each half into three slices lengthwise. Place the banana slices on two slices of bread and top with the remaining slices of bread (buttered side up) to make two sandwiches. Cut the sandwiches in half (triangles or rectangles) – this will help them all fit in the air fryer at once. Transfer the sandwiches to the air fryer.
3. Air-fry at 370°F for 5 minutes. Flip the sandwiches over and air-fry for another 2 to 3 minutes, or until the top bread slices are nicely browned. Pour yourself a glass of milk or a midnight nightcap while the sandwiches cool slightly and enjoy!

Dark Chocolate Peanut Butter S'mores

Servings: 4
Cooking Time: 6 Minutes

Ingredients:
- 4 graham cracker sheets
- 4 marshmallows
- 4 teaspoons chunky peanut butter
- 4 ounces dark chocolate
- ½ teaspoon ground cinnamon

Directions:
1. Preheat the air fryer to 390°F. Break the graham crackers in half so you have 8 pieces.
2. Place 4 pieces of graham cracker on the bottom of the air fryer. Top each with one of the marshmallows and bake for 6 or 7 minutes, or until the marshmallows have a golden brown center.
3. While cooking, slather each of the remaining graham crackers with 1 teaspoon peanut butter.
4. When baking completes, carefully remove each of the graham crackers, add 1 ounce of dark chocolate on top of the marshmallow, and lightly sprinkle with cinnamon. Top with the remaining peanut butter graham cracker to make the sandwich. Serve immediately.

Sugared Pizza Dough Dippers With Raspberry Cream Cheese Dip

Servings: 10

Cooking Time: 8 Minutes

Ingredients:

- 1 pound pizza dough*
- ½ cup butter, melted
- ¾ to 1 cup sugar
- Raspberry Cream Cheese Dip
- 4 ounces cream cheese, softened
- 2 tablespoons powdered sugar
- ½ teaspoon almond extract or almond paste
- 1½ tablespoons milk
- ¼ cup raspberry preserves
- fresh raspberries

Directions:

1. Cut the ingredients in half or save half of the dough for another recipe.

2. When you're ready to make your sugared dough dippers, remove your pizza dough from the refrigerator at least 1 hour prior to baking and let it sit on the counter, covered gently with plastic wrap.

3. Roll the dough into two 15-inch logs. Cut each log into 20 slices and roll each slice so that it is 3- to 3½-inches long. Cut each slice in half and twist the dough halves together 3 to 4 times. Place the twisted dough on a cookie sheet, brush with melted butter and sprinkle sugar over the dough twists.

4. Preheat the air fryer to 350°F.

5. Brush the bottom of the air fryer basket with a little melted butter. Air-fry the dough twists in batches. Place 8 to 12 (depending on the size of your air fryer) in the air fryer basket.

6. Air-fry for 6 minutes. Turn the dough strips over and brush the other side with butter. Air-fry for an additional 2 minutes.

7. While the dough twists are cooking, make the cream cheese and raspberry dip. Whip the cream cheese with a hand mixer until fluffy. Add the powdered sugar, almond extract and milk, and beat until smooth. Fold in the raspberry preserves and transfer to a serving dish.

8. As the batches of dough twists are complete, place them into a shallow dish. Brush with more melted butter and generously coat with sugar, shaking the dish to cover both sides. Serve the sugared dough dippers warm with the raspberry cream cheese dip on the side. Garnish with fresh raspberries.

Air-fried Beignets

Servings: 24
Cooking Time: 5 Minutes

Ingredients:

- ¾ cup lukewarm water (about 90°F)
- ¼ cup sugar
- 1 generous teaspoon active dry yeast (½ envelope)
- 3½ to 4 cups all-purpose flour
- ½ teaspoon salt
- 2 tablespoons unsalted butter, room temperature and cut into small pieces
- 1 egg, lightly beaten
- ½ cup evaporated milk
- ¼ cup melted butter
- 1 cup confectioners' sugar
- chocolate sauce or raspberry sauce, to dip

Directions:

1. Combine the lukewarm water, a pinch of the sugar and the yeast in a bowl and let it proof for 5 minutes. It should froth a little. If it doesn't froth, your yeast is not active and you should start again with new yeast.

2. Combine 3½ cups of the flour, salt, 2 tablespoons of butter and the remaining sugar in

a large bowl, or in the bowl of a stand mixer. Add the egg, evaporated milk and yeast mixture to the bowl and mix with a wooden spoon (or the paddle attachment of the stand mixer) until the dough comes together in a sticky ball. Add a little more flour if necessary to get the dough to form. Transfer the dough to an oiled bowl, cover with plastic wrap or a clean kitchen towel and let it rise in a warm place for at least 2 hours or until it has doubled in size. Longer is better for flavor development and you can even let the dough rest in the refrigerator overnight (just remember to bring it to room temperature before proceeding with the recipe).

3. Roll the dough out to ½-inch thickness. Cut the dough into rectangular or diamond-shaped pieces. You can make the beignets any size you like, but this recipe will give you 24 (2-inch x 3-inch) rectangles.

4. Preheat the air fryer to 350°F.

5. Brush the beignets on both sides with some of the melted butter and air-fry in batches at 350°F for 5 minutes, turning them over halfway through if desired. (They will brown on all sides without being flipped, but flipping them will brown them more evenly.)

6. As soon as the beignets are finished, transfer them to a plate or baking sheet and dust with the confectioners' sugar. Serve warm with a chocolate or raspberry sauce.

Hasselback Apple Crisp

Servings: 4
Cooking Time: 20 Minutes

Ingredients:
- 2 large Gala apples, peeled, cored and cut in half

- ¼ cup butter, melted
- ½ teaspoon ground cinnamon
- 2 tablespoons sugar
- Topping
- 3 tablespoons butter, melted
- 2 tablespoons brown sugar
- ¼ cup chopped pecans
- 2 tablespoons rolled oats*
- 1 tablespoon flour*
- vanilla ice cream
- caramel sauce

Directions:

1. Place the apples cut side down on a cutting board. Slicing from stem end to blossom end, make 8 to 10 slits down the apple halves but only slice three quarters of the way through the apple, not all the way through to the cutting board.

2. Preheat the air fryer to 330°F and pour a little water into the bottom of the air fryer drawer. (This will help prevent the grease that drips into the bottom drawer from burning and smoking.)

3. Transfer the apples to the air fryer basket, flat side down. Combine ¼ cup of melted butter, cinnamon and sugar in a small bowl. Brush this butter mixture onto the apples and air-fry at 330°F for 15 minutes. Baste the apples several times with the butter mixture during the cooking process.

4. While the apples are air-frying, make the filling. Combine 3 tablespoons of melted butter with the brown sugar, pecans, rolled oats and flour in a bowl. Stir with a fork until the mixture resembles small crumbles.

5. When the timer on the air fryer is up, spoon the topping down the center of the apples. Air-fry at 330°F for an additional 5 minutes.

6. Transfer the apples to a serving plate and serve with vanilla ice cream and caramel sauce.

Thumbprint Sugar Cookies

Servings: 10
Cooking Time: 8 Minutes

Ingredients:

- 2½ tablespoons butter
- ⅓ cup cane sugar
- 1 teaspoon pure vanilla extract
- 1 large egg
- 1 cup all-purpose flour
- ½ teaspoon baking soda
- ¼ teaspoon salt
- 10 chocolate kisses

Directions:

1. Preheat the air fryer to 350°F.
2. In a large bowl, cream the butter with the sugar and vanilla. Whisk in the egg and set aside.
3. In a separate bowl, mix the flour, baking soda, and salt. Then gently mix the dry ingredients into the wet. Portion the dough into 10 balls; then press down on each with the bottom of a cup to create a flat cookie.
4. Liberally spray the metal trivet of an air fryer basket with olive oil mist.
5. Place the cookies in the air fryer basket on the trivet and cook for 8 minutes or until the tops begin to lightly brown.
6. Remove and immediately press the chocolate kisses into the tops of the cookies while still warm.
7. Let cool 5 minutes and then enjoy.

Almond-roasted Pears

Servings: 4
Cooking Time: 15 Minutes

Ingredients:

- Yogurt Topping
- 1 container vanilla Greek yogurt (5–6 ounces)
- ¼ teaspoon almond flavoring
- 2 whole pears
- ¼ cup crushed Biscoff cookies (approx. 4 cookies)
- 1 tablespoon sliced almonds
- 1 tablespoon butter

Directions:

1. Stir almond flavoring into yogurt and set aside while preparing pears.
2. Halve each pear and spoon out the core.
3. Place pear halves in air fryer basket.
4. Stir together the cookie crumbs and almonds. Place a quarter of this mixture into the hollow of each pear half.
5. Cut butter into 4 pieces and place one piece on top of crumb mixture in each pear.
6. Cook at 360°F for 15 minutes or until pears have cooked through but are still slightly firm.
7. Serve pears warm with a dollop of yogurt topping.

Black And Blue Clafoutis

Servings: 2
Cooking Time: 15minutes

Ingredients:

- 6-inch pie pan
- 3 large eggs
- ½ cup sugar
- 1 teaspoon vanilla extract
- 2 tablespoons butter, melted 1 cup milk
- ½ cup all-purpose flour*
- 1 cup blackberries
- 1 cup blueberries
- 2 tablespoons confectioners' sugar

Directions:

1. Preheat the air fryer to 320°F.

2. Combine the eggs and sugar in a bowl and whisk vigorously until smooth, lighter in color and well combined. Add the vanilla extract, butter and milk and whisk together well. Add the flour and whisk just until no lumps or streaks of white remain.

3. Scatter half the blueberries and blackberries in a greased (6-inch) pie pan or cake pan. Pour half of the batter (about 1¼ cups) on top of the berries and transfer the tart pan to the air fryer basket. You can use an aluminum foil sling to help with this by taking a long piece of aluminum foil, folding it in half lengthwise twice until it is roughly 26-inches by 3-inches. Place this under the pie dish and hold the ends of the foil to move the pie dish in and out of the air fryer basket. Tuck the ends of the foil beside the pie dish while it cooks in the air fryer.

4. Air-fry at 320°F for 15 minutes or until the clafoutis has puffed up and is still a little jiggly in the center. Remove the clafoutis from the air fryer, invert it onto a plate and let it cool while you bake the second batch. Serve the clafoutis warm, dusted with confectioners' sugar on top.

Baked Apple

Servings: 6
Cooking Time: 20 Minutes

Ingredients:

- 3 small Honey Crisp or other baking apples
- 3 tablespoons maple syrup
- 3 tablespoons chopped pecans
- 1 tablespoon firm butter, cut into 6 pieces

Directions:

1. Put ½ cup water in the drawer of the air fryer.
2. Wash apples well and dry them.

3. Split apples in half. Remove core and a little of the flesh to make a cavity for the pecans.
4. Place apple halves in air fryer basket, cut side up.
5. Spoon 1½ teaspoons pecans into each cavity.
6. Spoon ½ tablespoon maple syrup over pecans in each apple.
7. Top each apple with ½ teaspoon butter.
8. Cook at 360°F for 20 minutes, until apples are tender.

Cherry Hand Pies

Servings: 8
Cooking Time: 8 Minutes

Ingredients:

- 4 cups frozen or canned pitted tart cherries (if using canned, drain and pat dry)
- 2 teaspoons lemon juice
- ½ cup sugar
- ¼ cup cornstarch
- 1 teaspoon vanilla extract
- 1 Basic Pie Dough (see the preceding recipe) or store-bought pie dough

Directions:

1. In a medium saucepan, place the cherries and lemon juice and cook over medium heat for 10 minutes, or until the cherries begin to break down.
2. In a small bowl, stir together the sugar and cornstarch. Pour the sugar mixture into the cherries, stirring constantly. Cook the cherry mixture over low heat for 2 to 3 minutes, or until thickened. Remove from the heat and stir in the vanilla extract. Allow the cherry mixture to cool to room temperature, about 30 minutes.
3. Meanwhile, bring the pie dough to room temperature. Divide the dough into 8 equal pieces. Roll out the dough to ¼-inch thickness in circles.

Place ¼ cup filling in the center of each rolled dough. Fold the dough to create a half-circle. Using a fork, press around the edges to seal the hand pies. Pierce the top of the pie with a fork for steam release while cooking. Continue until 8 hand pies are formed.

4. Preheat the air fryer to 350°F.

5. Place a single layer of hand pies in the air fryer basket and spray with cooking spray. Cook for 8 to 10 minutes or until golden brown and cooked through.

Cheesecake Wontons

Servings:16

Cooking Time: 6 Minutes

Ingredients:

*   ¼ cup Regular or low-fat cream cheese (not fat-free)
*   2 tablespoons Granulated white sugar
*   1½ tablespoons Egg yolk
*   ¼ teaspoon Vanilla extract
*   ⅛ teaspoon Table salt
*   1½ tablespoons All-purpose flour
*   16 Wonton wrappers (vegetarian, if a concern)
*   Vegetable oil spray

Directions:

1. Preheat the air fryer to 400°F.

2. Using a flatware fork, mash the cream cheese, sugar, egg yolk, and vanilla in a small bowl until smooth. Add the salt and flour and continue mashing until evenly combined.

3. Set a wonton wrapper on a clean, dry work surface so that one corner faces you (so that it looks like a diamond on your work surface). Set 1 teaspoon of the cream cheese mixture in the middle of the wrapper but just above a horizontal line that would divide the wrapper in half. Dip your clean finger in water and run it along the edges of the wrapper. Fold the corner closest to you up and over the filling, lining it up with the corner farthest from you, thereby making a stuffed triangle. Press gently to seal. Wet the two triangle tips nearest you, then fold them up and together over the filling. Gently press together to seal and fuse. Set aside and continue making more stuffed wontons, 11 more for the small batch, 15 more for the medium batch, or 23 more for the large one.

4. Lightly coat the stuffed wrappers on all sides with vegetable oil spray. Set them with the fused corners up in the basket with as much air space between them as possible. Air-fry undisturbed for 6 minutes, or until golden brown and crisp.

5. Gently dump the contents of the basket onto a wire rack. Cool for at least 5 minutes before serving.

Chocolate Soufflés

Servings: 2

Cooking Time: 14 Minutes

Ingredients:

*   butter and sugar for greasing the ramekins
*   3 ounces semi-sweet chocolate, chopped
*   ¼ cup unsalted butter
*   2 eggs, yolks and white separated
*   3 tablespoons sugar
*   ½ teaspoon pure vanilla extract
*   2 tablespoons all-purpose flour
*   powdered sugar, for dusting the finished soufflés
*   heavy cream, for serving

Directions:

1. Butter and sugar two 6-ounce ramekins. (Butter the ramekins and then coat the butter

with sugar by shaking it around in the ramekin and dumping out any excess.)

2. Melt the chocolate and butter together, either in the microwave or in a double boiler. In a separate bowl, beat the egg yolks vigorously. Add the sugar and the vanilla extract and beat well again. Drizzle in the chocolate and butter, mixing well. Stir in the flour, combining until there are no lumps.

3. Preheat the air fryer to 330°F.

4. In a separate bowl, whisk the egg whites to soft peak stage (the point at which the whites can almost stand up on the end of your whisk). Fold the whipped egg whites into the chocolate mixture gently and in stages.

5. Transfer the batter carefully to the buttered ramekins, leaving about ½-inch at the top. (You may have a little extra batter, depending on how airy the batter is, so you might be able to squeeze out a third soufflé if you want to.) Place the ramekins into the air fryer basket and air-fry for 14 minutes. The soufflés should have risen nicely and be brown on top. (Don't worry if the top gets a little dark – you'll be covering it with powdered sugar in the next step.)

6. Dust with powdered sugar and serve immediately with heavy cream to pour over the top at the table.

Honey-pecan Yogurt Cake

Servings: 6
Cooking Time: 18-24 Minutes

Ingredients:

- 1 cup plus 3½ tablespoons All-purpose flour
- ¼ teaspoon Baking powder
- ¼ teaspoon Baking soda
- ¼ teaspoon Table salt
- 5 tablespoons Plain full-fat, low-fat, or fat-free Greek yogurt
- 5 tablespoons Honey
- 5 tablespoons Pasteurized egg substitute, such as Egg Beaters
- 2 teaspoons Vanilla extract
- ⅔ cup Chopped pecans
- Baking spray (see here)

Directions:

1. Preheat the air fryer to 325°F (or 330°F, if the closest setting).

2. Mix the flour, baking powder, baking soda, and salt in a small bowl until well combined.

3. Using an electric hand mixer at medium speed , beat the yogurt, honey, egg substitute or egg, and vanilla in a medium bowl until smooth, about 2 minutes, scraping down the inside of the bowl once or twice.

4. Turn off the mixer; scrape down and remove the beaters. Fold in the flour mixture with a rubber spatula, just until all of the flour has been moistened. Fold in the pecans until they are evenly distributed in the mixture.

5. Use the baking spray to generously coat the inside of a 6-inch round cake pan for a small batch, a 7-inch round cake pan for a medium batch, or an 8-inch round cake pan for a large batch. Scrape and spread the batter into the pan, smoothing the batter out to an even layer.

6. Set the pan in the basket and air-fry for 18 minutes for a 6-inch layer, 22 minutes for a 7-inch layer, or 24 minutes for an 8-inch layer, or until a toothpick or cake tester inserted into the center of the cake comes out clean. Start checking it at the 15-minute mark to know where you are.

7. Use hot pads or silicone baking mitts to transfer the cake pan to a wire rack. Cool for 5

minutes. To unmold, set a cutting board over the baking pan and invert both the board and the pan. Lift the still-warm pan off the cake layer. Set the wire rack on top of that layer and invert all of it with the cutting board so that the cake layer is now right side up on the wire rack. Remove the cutting board and continue cooling the cake for at least 10 minutes or to room temperature, about 30 minutes, before slicing into wedges.

Brownies After Dark

Servings: 4
Cooking Time: 13 Minutes

Ingredients:

* 1 egg
* ½ cup granulated sugar
* ¼ teaspoon salt
* ½ teaspoon vanilla
* ¼ cup butter, melted
* ¼ cup flour, plus 2 tablespoons
* ¼ cup cocoa
* cooking spray
* Optional
* vanilla ice cream
* caramel sauce
* whipped cream

Directions:

1. Beat together egg, sugar, salt, and vanilla until light.
2. Add melted butter and mix well.
3. Stir in flour and cocoa.
4. Spray 6 x 6-inch baking pan lightly with cooking spray.
5. Spread batter in pan and cook at 330°F for 13 minutes. Cool and cut into 4 large squares or 16 small brownie bites.

Cinnamon Sugar Banana Rolls

Servings: 6
Cooking Time: 8 Minutes

Ingredients:

* ¼ cup Granulated white sugar
* 2 teaspoons Ground cinnamon
* 2 tablespoons Peach or apricot jam or orange marmalade
* 6 Spring roll wrappers, thawed if necessary
* 2 Ripe banana(s), peeled and cut into 3-inch-long sections
* 1 Large egg, well beaten
* Vegetable oil spray

Directions:

1. Preheat the air fryer to 400°F.
2. Stir the sugar and cinnamon in a small bowl until well combined. Stir the jam or marmalade with a fork to loosen it up.
3. Set a spring roll wrapper on a clean, dry work surface. Roll a banana section in the sugar mixture until evenly and well coated. Set the coated banana along one edge of the wrapper. Top it with about 1 teaspoon of the jam or marmalade. Fold the sides of the wrapper perpendicular to the banana up and over the banana, partially covering it. Brush beaten egg over the side of the wrapper farthest from the banana. Starting with the banana, roll the wrapper closed, ending at the part with the beaten egg. Press gently to seal. Set the roll aside seam side down and continue filling and rolling the remaining wrappers in the same way.
4. Lightly coat the wrappers with vegetable oil spray. Set them seam side down in the basket with as much air space between them as possible. Air-fry undisturbed for 8 minutes, or until crisp and golden brown.

5. Use kitchen tongs to gently transfer the rolls to a wire rack. Cool for at least 5 minutes or up to 30 minutes before serving.

Honey-roasted Mixed Nuts

Servings: 8
Cooking Time: 15 Minutes

Ingredients:
- ½ cup raw, shelled pistachios
- ½ cup raw almonds
- 1 cup raw walnuts
- 2 tablespoons filtered water
- 2 tablespoons honey
- 1 tablespoon vegetable oil
- 2 tablespoons sugar
- ½ teaspoon salt

Directions:
1. Preheat the air fryer to 300°F.
2. Lightly spray an air-fryer-safe pan with olive oil; then place the pistachios, almonds, and walnuts inside the pan and place the pan inside the air fryer basket.
3. Cook for 15 minutes, shaking the basket every 5 minutes to rotate the nuts.
4. While the nuts are roasting, boil the water in a small pan and stir in the honey and oil. Continue to stir while cooking until the water begins to evaporate and a thick sauce is formed. Note: The sauce should stick to the back of a wooden spoon when mixed. Turn off the heat.
5. Remove the nuts from the air fryer (cooking should have just completed) and spoon the nuts into the stovetop pan. Use a spatula to coat the nuts with the honey syrup.
6. Line a baking sheet with parchment paper and spoon the nuts onto the sheet. Lightly sprinkle the sugar and salt over the nuts and let cool in the refrigerator for at least 2 hours.
7. When the honey and sugar have hardened, store the nuts in an airtight container in the refrigerator.

Nutella® Torte

Servings: 6
Cooking Time: 55 Minutes

Ingredients:
- ¼ cup unsalted butter, softened
- ½ cup sugar
- 2 eggs
- 1 teaspoon vanilla
- 1¼ cups Nutella® (or other chocolate hazelnut spread), divided
- ¼ cup flour
- 1 teaspoon baking powder
- ¼ teaspoon salt
- dark chocolate fudge topping
- coarsely chopped toasted hazelnuts

Directions:
1. Cream the butter and sugar together with an electric hand mixer until light and fluffy. Add the eggs, vanilla, and ¾ cup of the Nutella® and mix until combined. Combine the flour, baking powder and salt together, and add these dry ingredients to the butter mixture, beating for 1 minute.
2. Preheat the air fryer to 350°F.
3. Grease a 7-inch cake pan with butter and then line the bottom of the pan with a circle of parchment paper. Grease the parchment paper circle as well. Pour the batter into the prepared cake pan and wrap the pan completely with aluminum foil. Lower the pan into the air fryer basket with an aluminum sling (fold a piece of

aluminum foil into a strip about 2-inches wide by 24-inches long). Fold the ends of the aluminum foil over the top of the dish before returning the basket to the air fryer. Air-fry for 30 minutes. Remove the foil and air-fry for another 25 minutes.

4. Remove the cake from air fryer and let it cool for 10 minutes. Invert the cake onto a plate, remove the parchment paper and invert the cake back onto a serving platter. While the cake is still warm, spread the remaining ½ cup of Nutella® over the top of the cake. Melt the dark chocolate fudge in the microwave for about 10 seconds so it melts enough to be pourable. Drizzle the sauce on top of the cake in a zigzag motion. Turn the cake 90 degrees and drizzle more sauce in zigzags perpendicular to the first zigzags. Garnish the edges of the torte with the toasted hazelnuts and serve.

Donut Holes

Servings: 13
Cooking Time: 12 Minutes

Ingredients:

- 6 tablespoons Granulated white sugar
- 1½ tablespoons Butter, melted and cooled
- 2 tablespoons (or 1 small egg, well beaten) Pasteurized egg substitute, such as Egg Beaters
- 6 tablespoons Regular or low-fat sour cream (not fat-free)
- ¾ teaspoon Vanilla extract
- 1⅔ cups All-purpose flour
- ¾ teaspoon Baking powder
- ¼ teaspoon Table salt
- Vegetable oil spray

Directions:

1. Preheat the air fryer to 350°F .

2. Whisk the sugar and melted butter in a medium bowl until well combined. Whisk in the egg substitute or egg , then the sour cream and vanilla until smooth. Remove the whisk and stir in the flour, baking powder, and salt with a wooden spoon just until a soft dough forms.

3. Use 2 tablespoons of this dough to create a ball between your clean palms. Set it aside and continue making balls: 8 more for the small batch, 12 more for the medium batch, or 17 more for the large one.

4. Coat the balls in the vegetable oil spray, then set them in the basket with as much air space between them as possible. Even a fraction of an inch will be enough, but they should not touch. Air-fry undisturbed for 12 minutes, or until browned and cooked through. A toothpick inserted into the center of a ball should come out clean.

5. Pour the contents of the basket onto a wire rack. Cool for at least 5 minutes before serving.

Apple Crisp

Servings: 4

Cooking Time: 16 Minutes

Ingredients:

- Filling
- 3 Granny Smith apples, thinly sliced (about 4 cups)
- ¼ teaspoon ground cinnamon
- ⅛ teaspoon salt
- 1½ teaspoons lemon juice
- 2 tablespoons honey
- 1 tablespoon brown sugar
- cooking spray
- Crumb Topping
- 2 tablespoons oats
- 2 tablespoons oat bran
- 2 tablespoons cooked quinoa
- 2 tablespoons chopped walnuts
- 2 tablespoons brown sugar
- 2 teaspoons coconut oil

Directions:

1. Combine all filling ingredients and stir well so that apples are evenly coated.

2. Spray air fryer baking pan with nonstick cooking spray and spoon in the apple mixture.

3. Cook at 360°F for 5minutes. Stir well, scooping up from the bottom to mix apples and sauce.

4. At this point, the apples should be crisp-tender. Continue cooking in 3-minute intervals until apples are as soft as you like.

5. While apples are cooking, combine all topping ingredients in a small bowl. Stir until coconut oil mixes in well and distributes evenly. If your coconut oil is cold, it may be easier to mix in by hand.

6. When apples are cooked to your liking, sprinkle crumb mixture on top. Cook at 360°F for 8 minutes or until crumb topping is golden brown and crispy.

VEGETARIANS RECIPES

Black Bean Empanadas

Servings: 12
Cooking Time: 35 Minutes

Ingredients:

- 1½ cups all-purpose flour
- 1 cup whole-wheat flour
- 1 teaspoon salt
- ½ cup cold unsalted butter
- 1 egg
- ½ cup milk
- One 14.5-ounce can black beans, drained and rinsed
- ¼ cup chopped cilantro
- 1 cup shredded purple cabbage
- 1 cup shredded Monterey jack cheese
- ¼ cup salsa

Directions:

1. In a food processor, place the all-purpose flour, whole-wheat flour, salt, and butter into processor and process for 2 minutes, scraping down the sides of the food processor every 30 seconds. Add in the egg and blend for 30 seconds. Using the pulse button, add in the milk 1 tablespoon at a time, or until dough is moist enough to handle and be rolled into a ball. Let the dough rest at room temperature for 30 minutes.

2. Meanwhile, in a large bowl, mix together the black beans, cilantro, cabbage, Monterey Jack cheese, and salsa.

3. On a floured surface, cut the dough in half; then form a ball and cut each ball into 6 equal pieces, totaling 12 equal pieces. Work with one piece at a time, and cover the remaining dough with a towel.

4. Roll out a piece of dough into a 6-inch round, much like a tortilla, ¼ inch thick. Place 4 tablespoons of filling in the center of the round, and fold over to form a half-circle. Using a fork, crimp the edges together and pierce the top for air holes. Repeat with the remaining dough and filling.

5. Preheat the air fryer to 350°F.

6. Working in batches, place 3 to 4 empanadas in the air fryer basket and spray with cooking spray. Cook for 4 minutes, flip over the empanadas and spray with cooking spray, and cook another 4 minutes.

Asparagus, Mushroom And Cheese Soufflés

Servings: 3
Cooking Time: 21 Minutes

Ingredients:

- butter
- grated Parmesan cheese
- 3 button mushrooms, thinly sliced
- 8 spears asparagus, sliced ½-inch long
- 1 teaspoon olive oil
- 1 tablespoon butter
- 4½ teaspoons flour
- pinch paprika
- pinch ground nutmeg
- salt and freshly ground black pepper
- ½ cup milk
- ½ cup grated Gruyère cheese or other Swiss cheese (about 2 ounces)
- 2 eggs, separated

Directions:

1. Butter three 6-ounce ramekins and dust with grated Parmesan cheese. (Butter the ramekins and then coat the butter with Parmesan by shaking it around in the ramekin and dumping out any excess.)

2. Preheat the air fryer to 400°F.

3. Toss the mushrooms and asparagus in a bowl with the olive oil. Transfer the vegetables to the air fryer and air-fry for 7 minutes, shaking the basket once or twice to redistribute the Ingredients while they cook.

4. While the vegetables are cooking, make the soufflé base. Melt the butter in a saucepan on the stovetop over medium heat. Add the flour, stir and cook for a minute or two. Add the paprika, nutmeg, salt and pepper. Whisk in the milk and bring the mixture to a simmer to thicken. Remove the pan from the heat and add the cheese, stirring to melt. Let the mixture cool for just a few minutes and then whisk the egg yolks in, one at a time. Stir in the cooked mushrooms and asparagus. Let this soufflé base cool.

5. In a separate bowl, whisk the egg whites to soft peak stage (the point at which the whites can almost stand up on the end of your whisk). Fold the whipped egg whites into the soufflé base, adding a little at a time.

6. Preheat the air fryer to 330°F.

7. Transfer the batter carefully to the buttered ramekins, leaving about ½-inch at the top. Place the ramekins into the air fryer basket and air-fry for 14 minutes. The soufflés should have risen nicely and be brown on top. Serve immediately.

Mushroom, Zucchini And Black Bean Burgers

Servings: 4

Cooking Time: 18 Minutes

Ingredients:

- 1 cup diced zucchini, (about ½ medium zucchini)
- 1 tablespoon olive oil
- salt and freshly ground black pepper
- 1 cup chopped brown mushrooms (about 3 ounces)
- 1 small clove garlic
- 1 (15-ounce) can black beans, drained and rinsed
- 1 teaspoon lemon zest
- 1 tablespoon chopped fresh cilantro
- ½ cup plain breadcrumbs
- 1 egg, beaten
- ½ teaspoon salt
- freshly ground black pepper
- whole-wheat pita bread, burger buns or brioche buns
- mayonnaise, tomato, avocado and lettuce, for serving

Directions:

1. Preheat the air fryer to 400°F.

2. Toss the zucchini with the olive oil, season with salt and freshly ground black pepper and air-fry for 6 minutes, shaking the basket once or twice while it cooks.

3. Transfer the zucchini to a food processor with the mushrooms, garlic and black beans and process until still a little chunky but broken down and pasty. Transfer the mixture to a bowl. Add the lemon zest, cilantro, breadcrumbs and egg and mix well. Season again with salt and freshly

ground black pepper. Shape the mixture into four burger patties and refrigerate for at least 15 minutes.

4.   Preheat the air fryer to 370°F. Transfer two of the veggie burgers to the air fryer basket and air-fry for 12 minutes, flipping the burgers gently halfway through the cooking time. Keep the burgers warm by loosely tenting them with foil while you cook the remaining two burgers. Return the first batch of burgers back into the air fryer with the second batch for the last two minutes of cooking to re-heat.

5.   Serve on toasted whole-wheat pita bread, burger buns or brioche buns with some mayonnaise, tomato, avocado and lettuce.

Broccoli Cheddar Stuffed Potatoes

Servings: 2
Cooking Time: 42 Minutes

Ingredients:
*   2 large russet potatoes, scrubbed
*   1 tablespoon olive oil
*   salt and freshly ground black pepper
*   2 tablespoons butter
*   ¼ cup sour cream
*   3 tablespoons half-and-half (or milk)
*   1¼ cups grated Cheddar cheese, divided
*   ¾ teaspoon salt
*   freshly ground black pepper
*   1 cup frozen baby broccoli florets, thawed and drained

Directions:
1.   Preheat the air fryer to 400°F.
2.   Rub the potatoes all over with olive oil and season generously with salt and freshly ground black pepper. Transfer the potatoes into the air

fryer basket and air-fry for 30 minutes, turning the potatoes over halfway through the cooking process.

3.   Remove the potatoes from the air fryer and let them rest for 5 minutes. Cut a large oval out of the top of both potatoes. Leaving half an inch of potato flesh around the edge of the potato, scoop the inside of the potato out and into a large bowl to prepare the potato filling. Mash the scooped potato filling with a fork and add the butter, sour cream, half-and-half, 1 cup of the grated Cheddar cheese, salt and pepper to taste. Mix well and then fold in the broccoli florets.

4.   Stuff the hollowed out potato shells with the potato and broccoli mixture. Mound the filling high in the potatoes – you will have more filling than room in the potato shells.

5.   Transfer the stuffed potatoes back to the air fryer basket and air-fry at 360°F for 10 minutes. Sprinkle the remaining Cheddar cheese on top of each stuffed potato, lower the heat to 330°F and air-fry for an additional minute or two to melt cheese.

Roasted Vegetable, Brown Rice And Black Bean Burrito

Servings: 2
Cooking Time: 20 Minutes

Ingredients:
*   ½ zucchini, sliced ¼-inch thick
*   ½ red onion, sliced
*   1 yellow bell pepper, sliced
*   2 teaspoons olive oil
*   salt and freshly ground black pepper
*   2 burrito size flour tortillas
*   1 cup grated pepper jack cheese
*   ½ cup cooked brown rice

- ½ cup canned black beans, drained and rinsed
- ¼ teaspoon ground cumin
- 1 tablespoon chopped fresh cilantro
- fresh salsa, guacamole and sour cream, for serving

Directions:

1. Preheat the air fryer to 400°F.

2. Toss the vegetables in a bowl with the olive oil, salt and freshly ground black pepper. Air-fry at 400°F for 12 to 15 minutes, shaking the basket a few times during the cooking process. The vegetables are done when they are cooked to your liking.

3. In the meantime, start building the burritos. Lay the tortillas out on the counter. Sprinkle half of the cheese in the center of the tortillas. Combine the rice, beans, cumin and cilantro in a bowl, season to taste with salt and freshly ground black pepper and then divide the mixture between the two tortillas. When the vegetables have finished cooking, transfer them to the two tortillas, placing the vegetables on top of the rice and beans. Sprinkle the remaining cheese on top and then roll the burritos up, tucking in the sides of the tortillas as you roll. Brush or spray the outside of the burritos with olive oil and transfer them to the air fryer.

4. Air-fry at 360°F for 8 minutes, turning them over when there are about 2 minutes left. The burritos will have slightly brown spots, but will still be pliable.

5. Serve with some fresh salsa, guacamole and sour cream.

Tandoori Paneer Naan Pizza

Servings: 4
Cooking Time: 10 Minutes

Ingredients:

- 6 tablespoons plain Greek yogurt, divided
- 1¼ teaspoons garam marsala, divided
- ½ teaspoon turmeric, divided
- ¼ teaspoon garlic powder
- ½ teaspoon paprika, divided
- ½ teaspoon black pepper, divided
- 3 ounces paneer, cut into small cubes
- 1 tablespoon extra-virgin olive oil
- 2 teaspoons minced garlic
- 4 cups baby spinach
- 2 tablespoons marinara sauce
- ¼ teaspoon salt
- 2 plain naan breads (approximately 6 inches in diameter)
- ½ cup shredded part-skim mozzarella cheese

Directions:

1. Preheat the air fryer to 350°F.

2. In a small bowl, mix 2 tablespoons of the yogurt, ½ teaspoon of the garam marsala, ¼ teaspoon of the turmeric, the garlic powder, ¼ teaspoon of the paprika, and ¼ teaspoon of the black pepper. Toss the paneer cubes in the mixture and let marinate for at least an hour.

3. Meanwhile, in a pan, heat the olive oil over medium heat. Add in the minced garlic and sauté for 1 minute. Stir in the spinach and begin to cook until it wilts. Add in the remaining 4 tablespoons of yogurt and the marinara sauce. Stir in the remaining ¾ teaspoon of garam masala, the remaining ¼ teaspoon of turmeric, the remaining ¼ teaspoon of paprika, the remaining ¼ teaspoon of black pepper, and the salt. Let simmer a minute or two, and then remove from the heat.

4. Equally divide the spinach mixture amongst the two naan breads. Place 1½ ounces of the marinated paneer on each naan.

5. Liberally spray the air fryer basket with olive oil mist.

6. Use a spatula to pick up one naan and place it in the air fryer basket.

7. Cook for 4 minutes, open the basket and sprinkle ¼ cup of mozzarella cheese on top, and cook another 4 minutes.

8. Remove from the air fryer and repeat with the remaining naan.

9. Serve warm.

Spicy Vegetable And Tofu Shake Fry

Servings: 4
Cooking Time: 17 Minutes

Ingredients:

- 4 teaspoons canola oil, divided
- 2 tablespoons rice wine vinegar
- 1 tablespoon sriracha chili sauce
- ¼ cup soy sauce*
- ½ teaspoon toasted sesame oil
- 1 teaspoon minced garlic
- 1 tablespoon minced fresh ginger
- 8 ounces extra firm tofu
- ½ cup vegetable stock or water
- 1 tablespoon honey
- 1 tablespoon cornstarch
- ½ red onion, chopped
- 1 red or yellow bell pepper, chopped
- 1 cup green beans, cut into 2-inch lengths
- 4 ounces mushrooms, sliced
- 2 scallions, sliced
- 2 tablespoons fresh cilantro leaves
- 2 teaspoons toasted sesame seeds

Directions:

1. Combine 1 tablespoon of the oil, vinegar, sriracha sauce, soy sauce, sesame oil, garlic and ginger in a small bowl. Cut the tofu into bite-sized cubes and toss the tofu in with the marinade while you prepare the other vegetables. When you are ready to start cooking, remove the tofu from the marinade and set it aside. Add the water, honey and cornstarch to the marinade and bring to a simmer on the stovetop, just until the sauce thickens. Set the sauce aside.

2. Preheat the air fryer to 400°F.

3. Toss the onion, pepper, green beans and mushrooms in a bowl with a little canola oil and season with salt. Air-fry at 400°F for 11 minutes, shaking the basket and tossing the vegetables every few minutes. When the vegetables are cooked to your preferred doneness, remove them from the air fryer and set aside.

4. Add the tofu to the air fryer basket and air-fry at 400°F for 6 minutes, shaking the basket a few times during the cooking process. Add the vegetables back to the basket and air-fry for another minute. Transfer the vegetables and tofu to a large bowl, add the scallions and cilantro leaves and toss with the sauce. Serve over rice with sesame seeds sprinkled on top.

Falafels

Servings: 12
Cooking Time: 10 Minutes

Ingredients:

- 1 pouch falafel mix
- 2–3 tablespoons plain breadcrumbs
- oil for misting or cooking spray

Directions:

1. Prepare falafel mix according to package directions.

2. Preheat air fryer to 390°F.

3. Place breadcrumbs in shallow dish or on wax paper.

4. Shape falafel mixture into 12 balls and flatten slightly. Roll in breadcrumbs to coat all sides and mist with oil or cooking spray.

5. Place falafels in air fryer basket in single layer and cook for 5minutes. Shake basket, and continue cooking for 5minutes, until they brown and are crispy.

Vegetable Hand Pies

Servings: 8

Cooking Time: 10 Minutes Per Batch

Ingredients:

- ¾ cup vegetable broth
- 8 ounces potatoes
- ¾ cup frozen chopped broccoli, thawed
- ¼ cup chopped mushrooms
- 1 tablespoon cornstarch
- 1 tablespoon milk
- 1 can organic flaky biscuits (8 large biscuits)
- oil for misting or cooking spray

Directions:

1. Place broth in medium saucepan over low heat.

2. While broth is heating, grate raw potato into a bowl of water to prevent browning. You will need ¾ cup grated potato.

3. Roughly chop the broccoli.

4. Drain potatoes and put them in the broth along with the broccoli and mushrooms. Cook on low for 5 minutes.

5. Dissolve cornstarch in milk, then stir the mixture into the broth. Cook about a minute, until mixture thickens a little. Remove from heat and cool slightly.

6. Separate each biscuit into 2 rounds. Divide vegetable mixture evenly over half the biscuit rounds, mounding filling in the center of each.

7. Top the four rounds with filling, then the other four rounds and crimp the edges together with a fork.

8. Spray both sides with oil or cooking spray and place 4 pies in a single layer in the air fryer basket.

9. Cook at 330°F for approximately 10 minutes.

10. Repeat with the remaining biscuits. The second batch may cook more quickly because the fryer will be hot.

Curried Potato, Cauliflower And Pea Turnovers

Servings: 4

Cooking Time: 40 Minutes

Ingredients:

- Dough:
- 2 cups all-purpose flour
- ½ teaspoon baking powder
- 1 teaspoon salt
- freshly ground black pepper
- ¼ teaspoon dried thyme
- ¼ cup canola oil
- ½ to ⅔ cup water
- Turnover Filling:
- 1 tablespoon canola or vegetable oil
- 1 onion, finely chopped
- 1 clove garlic, minced
- 1 tablespoon grated fresh ginger
- ½ teaspoon cumin seeds
- ½ teaspoon fennel seeds
- 1 teaspoon curry powder
- 2 russet potatoes, diced
- 2 cups cauliflower florets
- ½ cup frozen peas

- 2 tablespoons chopped fresh cilantro
- salt and freshly ground black pepper
- 2 tablespoons butter, melted
- mango chutney, for serving

Directions:

1. Start by making the dough. Combine the flour, baking powder, salt, pepper and dried thyme in a mixing bowl or the bowl of a stand mixer. Drizzle in the canola oil and pinch it together with your fingers to turn the flour into a crumby mixture. Stir in the water (enough to bring the dough together). Knead the dough for 5 minutes or so until it is smooth. Add a little more water or flour as needed. Let the dough rest while you make the turnover filling.

2. Preheat a large skillet on the stovetop over medium-high heat. Add the oil and sauté the onion until it starts to become tender – about 4 minutes. Add the garlic and ginger and continue to cook for another minute. Add the dried spices and toss everything to coat. Add the potatoes and cauliflower to the skillet and pour in 1½ cups of water. Simmer everything together for 20 to 25 minutes, or until the potatoes are soft and most of the water has evaporated. If the water has evaporated and the vegetables still need more time, just add a little water and continue to simmer until everything is tender. Stir well, crushing the potatoes and cauliflower a little as you do so. Stir in the peas and cilantro, season to taste with salt and freshly ground black pepper and set aside to cool.

3. Divide the dough into 4 balls. Roll the dough balls out into ¼-inch thick circles. Divide the cooled potato filling between the dough circles, placing a mound of the filling on one side of each piece of dough, leaving an empty border around the edge of the dough. Brush the edges of the dough with a little water and fold one edge of circle over the filling to meet the other edge of the circle, creating a half moon. Pinch the edges together with your fingers and then press the edge with the tines of a fork to decorate and seal.

4. Preheat the air fryer to 380°F.

5. Spray or brush the air fryer basket with oil. Brush the turnovers with the melted butter and place 2 turnovers into the air fryer basket. Air-fry for 15 minutes. Flip the turnovers over and air-fry for another 5 minutes. Repeat with the remaining 2 turnovers.

6. These will be very hot when they come out of the air fryer. Let them cool for at least 20 minutes before serving warm with mango chutney.

Eggplant Parmesan

Servings: 4
Cooking Time: 8 Minutes Per Batch

Ingredients:
- 1 medium eggplant, 6–8 inches long
- salt
- 1 large egg
- 1 tablespoon water
- ⅔ cup panko breadcrumbs
- ⅓ cup grated Parmesan cheese, plus more for serving
- 1 tablespoon Italian seasoning
- ¾ teaspoon oregano
- oil for misting or cooking spray
- 1 24-ounce jar marinara sauce
- 8 ounces spaghetti, cooked
- pepper

Directions:

1. Preheat air fryer to 390°F.

2. Leaving peel intact, cut eggplant into 8 round slices about ¾-inch thick. Salt to taste.

3. Beat egg and water in a shallow dish.

4. In another shallow dish, combine panko, Parmesan, Italian seasoning, and oregano.

5. Dip eggplant slices in egg wash and then crumbs, pressing lightly to coat.

6. Mist slices with oil or cooking spray.

7. Place 4 eggplant slices in air fryer basket and cook for 8 minutes, until brown and crispy.

8. While eggplant is cooking, heat marinara sauce.

9. Repeat step 7 to cook remaining eggplant slices.

10. To serve, place cooked spaghetti on plates and top with marinara and eggplant slices. At the table, pass extra Parmesan cheese and freshly ground black pepper.

Arancini With Marinara

Servings: 6
Cooking Time: 15 Minutes

Ingredients:
- 2 cups cooked rice
- 1 cup grated Parmesan cheese
- 1 egg, whisked
- ¼ teaspoon dried thyme
- ½ teaspoon dried oregano
- ½ teaspoon dried basil
- ½ teaspoon dried parsley
- 1 teaspoon salt
- ¼ teaspoon paprika
- 1 cup breadcrumbs
- 4 ounces mozzarella, cut into 24 cubes
- 2 cups marinara sauce

Directions:

1. In a large bowl, mix together the rice, Parmesan cheese, and egg.

2. In another bowl, mix together the thyme, oregano, basil, parsley, salt, paprika, and breadcrumbs.

3. Form 24 rice balls with the rice mixture. Use your thumb to make an indentation in the center and stuff 1 cube of mozzarella in the center of the rice; close the ball around the cheese.

4. Roll the rice balls in the seasoned breadcrumbs until all are coated.

5. Preheat the air fryer to 400°F.

6. Place the rice balls in the air fryer basket and coat with cooking spray. Cook for 8 minutes, shake the basket, and cook another 7 minutes.

7. Heat the marinara sauce in a saucepan until warm. Serve sauce as a dip for arancini.

Parmesan Portobello Mushroom Caps

Servings: 2
Cooking Time: 14 Minutes

Ingredients:
- ¼ cup flour*
- 1 egg, lightly beaten
- 1 cup seasoned breadcrumbs*
- 2 large portobello mushroom caps, stems and gills removed
- olive oil, in a spray bottle
- ½ cup tomato sauce
- ¾ cup grated mozzarella cheese
- 1 tablespoon grated Parmesan cheese
- 1 tablespoon chopped fresh basil or parsley

Directions:

1. Set up a dredging station with three shallow dishes. Place the flour in the first shallow dish, egg in the second dish and breadcrumbs in the

last dish. Dredge the mushrooms in flour, then dip them into the egg and finally press them into the breadcrumbs to coat on all sides. Spray both sides of the coated mushrooms with olive oil.

2. Preheat the air fryer to 400°F.

3. Air-fry the mushrooms at 400°F for 10 minutes, turning them over halfway through the cooking process.

4. Fill the underside of the mushrooms with the tomato sauce and then top the sauce with the mozzarella and Parmesan cheeses. Reset the air fryer temperature to 350°F and air-fry for an additional 4 minutes, until the cheese has melted and is slightly browned.

5. Serve the mushrooms with pasta tossed with tomato sauce and garnish with some chopped fresh basil or parsley.

Corn And Pepper Jack Chile Rellenos With Roasted Tomato Sauce

Servings: 3
Cooking Time: 30 Minutes

Ingredients:
- 3 Poblano peppers
- 1 cup all-purpose flour*
- salt and freshly ground black pepper
- 2 eggs, lightly beaten
- 1 cup plain breadcrumbs*
- olive oil, in a spray bottle
- Sauce
- 2 cups cherry tomatoes
- 1 Jalapeño pepper, halved and seeded
- 1 clove garlic
- ¼ red onion, broken into large pieces
- 1 tablespoon olive oil
- salt, to taste
- 2 tablespoons chopped fresh cilantro
- Filling
- olive oil
- ¼ red onion, finely chopped
- 1 teaspoon minced garlic
- 1 cup corn kernels, fresh or frozen
- 2 cups grated pepper jack cheese

Directions:
1. Start by roasting the peppers. Preheat the air fryer to 400°F. Place the peppers into the air fryer basket and air-fry at 400°F for 10 minutes, turning them over halfway through the cooking time. Remove the peppers from the basket and cover loosely with foil.

2. While the peppers are cooling, make the roasted tomato sauce. Place all sauce Ingredients except for the cilantro into the air fryer basket and air-fry at 400°F for 10 minutes, shaking the basket once or twice. When the sauce Ingredients have finished air-frying, transfer everything to a blender or food processor and blend or process to a smooth sauce, adding a little warm water to get the desired consistency. Season to taste with salt, add the cilantro and set aside.

3. While the sauce Ingredients are cooking in the air fryer, make the filling. Heat a skillet on the stovetop over medium heat. Add the olive oil and sauté the red onion and garlic for 4 to 5 minutes. Transfer the onion and garlic to a bowl, stir in the corn and cheese, and set aside.

4. Set up a dredging station with three shallow dishes. Place the flour, seasoned with salt and pepper, in the first shallow dish. Place the eggs in the second dish, and fill the third shallow dish with the breadcrumbs. When the peppers have cooled, carefully slice into one side of the pepper

to create an opening. Pull the seeds out of the peppers and peel away the skins, trying not to tear the pepper. Fill each pepper with some of the corn and cheese filling and close the pepper up again by folding one side of the opening over the other. Carefully roll each pepper in the seasoned flour, then into the egg and finally into the breadcrumbs to coat on all sides, trying not to let the pepper fall open. Spray the peppers on all sides with a little olive oil.

5. Air-fry two peppers at a time at 350°F for 6 minutes. Turn the peppers over and air-fry for another 4 minutes. Serve the peppers warm on a bed of the roasted tomato sauce.

Lentil Fritters

Servings: 9
Cooking Time: 12 Minutes

Ingredients:
- 1 cup cooked red lentils
- 1 cup riced cauliflower
- ½ medium zucchini, shredded (about 1 cup)
- ¼ cup finely chopped onion
- ¼ teaspoon salt
- ¼ teaspoon black pepper
- ½ teaspoon garlic powder
- ¼ teaspoon paprika
- 1 large egg
- ⅓ cup quinoa flour

Directions:
1. Preheat the air fryer to 370°F.
2. In a large bowl, mix the lentils, cauliflower, zucchini, onion, salt, pepper, garlic powder, and paprika. Mix in the egg and flour until a thick dough forms.
3. Using a large spoon, form the dough into 9 large fritters.

4. Liberally spray the air fryer basket with olive oil. Place the fritters into the basket, leaving space around each fritter so you can flip them.
5. Cook for 6 minutes, flip, and cook another 6 minutes.
6. Remove from the air fryer and repeat with the remaining fritters. Serve warm with desired sauce and sides.

Basic Fried Tofu

Servings: 4
Cooking Time: 17 Minutes

Ingredients:
- 14 ounces extra-firm tofu, drained and pressed
- 1 tablespoon sesame oil
- 2 tablespoons low-sodium soy sauce
- ¼ cup rice vinegar
- 1 tablespoon fresh grated ginger
- 1 clove garlic, minced
- 3 tablespoons cornstarch
- ¼ teaspoon black pepper
- ⅛ teaspoon salt

Directions:
1. Cut the tofu into 16 cubes. Set aside in a glass container with a lid.
2. In a medium bowl, mix the sesame oil, soy sauce, rice vinegar, ginger, and garlic. Pour over the tofu and secure the lid. Place in the refrigerator to marinate for an hour.
3. Preheat the air fryer to 350°F.
4. In a small bowl, mix the cornstarch, black pepper, and salt.
5. Transfer the tofu to a large bowl and discard the leftover marinade. Pour the cornstarch mixture over the tofu and toss until all the pieces are coated.

6. Liberally spray the air fryer basket with olive oil mist and set the tofu pieces inside. Allow space between the tofu so it can cook evenly. Cook in batches if necessary.

7. Cook 15 to 17 minutes, shaking the basket every 5 minutes to allow the tofu to cook evenly on all sides. When it's done cooking, the tofu will be crisped and browned on all sides.

8. Remove the tofu from the air fryer basket and serve warm.

Veggie Burgers

Servings: 4
Cooking Time: 15 Minutes

Ingredients:

- 2 cans black beans, rinsed and drained
- ½ cup cooked quinoa
- ½ cup shredded raw sweet potato
- ¼ cup diced red onion
- 2 teaspoons ground cumin
- 1 teaspoon coriander powder
- ½ teaspoon salt
- oil for misting or cooking spray
- 8 slices bread
- suggested toppings: lettuce, tomato, red onion, Pepper Jack cheese, guacamole

Directions:

1. In a medium bowl, mash the beans with a fork.

2. Add the quinoa, sweet potato, onion, cumin, coriander, and salt and mix well with the fork.

3. Shape into 4 patties, each ¾-inch thick.

4. Mist both sides with oil or cooking spray and also mist the basket.

5. Cook at 390°F for 15minutes.

6. Follow the recipe for Toast, Plain & Simple.

7. Pop the veggie burgers back in the air fryer for a minute or two to reheat if necessary.

8. Serve on the toast with your favorite burger toppings.

Tacos

Servings: 24
Cooking Time: 8 Minutes Per Batch

Ingredients:

- 1 24-count package 4-inch corn tortillas
- 1½ cups refried beans (about ¾ of a 15-ounce can)
- 4 ounces sharp Cheddar cheese, grated
- ½ cup salsa
- oil for misting or cooking spray

Directions:

1. Preheat air fryer to 390°F.

2. Wrap refrigerated tortillas in damp paper towels and microwave for 30 to 60 seconds to warm. If necessary, rewarm tortillas as you go to keep them soft enough to fold without breaking.

3. Working with one tortilla at a time, top with 1 tablespoon of beans, 1 tablespoon of grated cheese, and 1 teaspoon of salsa. Fold over and press down very gently on the center. Press edges firmly all around to seal. Spray both sides with oil or cooking spray.

4. Cooking in two batches, place half the tacos in the air fryer basket. To cook 12 at a time, you may need to stand them upright and lean some against the sides of basket. It's okay if they're crowded as long as you leave a little room for air to circulate around them.

5. Cook for 8 minutes or until golden brown and crispy.

6. Repeat steps 4 and 5 to cook remaining tacos.

Veggie Fried Rice

Servings: 4

Cooking Time: 25 Minutes

Ingredients:

- 1 cup cooked brown rice
- ⅓ cup chopped onion
- ½ cup chopped carrots
- ½ cup chopped bell peppers
- ½ cup chopped broccoli florets
- 3 tablespoons low-sodium soy sauce
- 1 tablespoon sesame oil
- 1 teaspoon ground ginger
- 1 teaspoon ground garlic powder
- ½ teaspoon black pepper
- ⅛ teaspoon salt
- 2 large eggs

Directions:

1. Preheat the air fryer to 370°F.
2. In a large bowl, mix together the brown rice, onions, carrots, bell pepper, and broccoli.
3. In a small bowl, whisk together the soy sauce, sesame oil, ginger, garlic powder, pepper, salt, and eggs.
4. Pour the egg mixture into the rice and vegetable mixture and mix together.
5. Liberally spray a 7-inch springform pan (or compatible air fryer dish) with olive oil. Add the rice mixture to the pan and cover with aluminum foil.
6. Place a metal trivet into the air fryer basket and set the pan on top. Cook for 15 minutes. Carefully remove the pan from basket, discard the foil, and mix the rice. Return the rice to the air fryer basket, turning down the temperature to 350°F and cooking another 10 minutes.
7. Remove and let cool 5 minutes. Serve warm.

Stuffed Zucchini Boats

Servings: 2

Cooking Time: 20 Minutes

Ingredients:

- olive oil
- ½ cup onion, finely chopped
- 1 clove garlic, finely minced
- ½ teaspoon dried oregano
- ¼ teaspoon dried thyme
- ¾ cup couscous
- 1½ cups chicken stock, divided
- 1 tomato, seeds removed and finely chopped
- ½ cup coarsely chopped Kalamata olives
- ½ cup grated Romano cheese
- ¼ cup pine nuts, toasted
- 1 tablespoon chopped fresh parsley
- 1 teaspoon salt
- freshly ground black pepper
- 1 egg, beaten
- 1 cup grated mozzarella cheese, divided
- 2 thick zucchini

Directions:

1. Preheat a sauté pan on the stovetop over medium-high heat. Add the olive oil and sauté the onion until it just starts to soften–about 4 minutes. Stir in the garlic, dried oregano and thyme. Add the couscous and sauté for just a minute. Add 1¼ cups of the chicken stock and simmer over low heat for 3 to 5 minutes, until liquid has been absorbed and the couscous is soft. Remove the pan from heat and set it aside to cool slightly.
2. Fluff the couscous and add the tomato, Kalamata olives, Romano cheese, pine nuts, parsley, salt and pepper. Mix well. Add the remaining chicken stock, the egg and ½ cup of

the mozzarella cheese. Stir to ensure everything is combined.

3. Cut each zucchini in half lengthwise. Then, trim each half of the zucchini into four 5-inch lengths. (Save the trimmed ends of the zucchini for another use.) Use a spoon to scoop out the center of the zucchini, leaving some flesh around the sides. Brush both sides of the zucchini with olive oil and season the cut side with salt and pepper.

4. Preheat the air fryer to 380°F.

5. Divide the couscous filling between the four zucchini boats. Use your hands to press the filling together and fill the inside of the zucchini. The filling should be mounded into the boats and rounded on top.

6. Transfer the zucchini boats to the air fryer basket and drizzle the stuffed zucchini boats with olive oil. Air-fry for 19 minutes. Then, sprinkle the remaining mozzarella cheese on top of the zucchini, pressing it down onto the filling lightly to prevent it from blowing around in the air fryer. Air-fry for one more minute to melt the cheese. Transfer the finished zucchini boats to a serving platter and garnish with the chopped parsley.

Vegetable Couscous

Servings: 4
Cooking Time: 10 Minutes

Ingredients:
- 4 ounces white mushrooms, sliced
- ½ medium green bell pepper, julienned
- 1 cup cubed zucchini
- ¼ small onion, slivered
- 1 stalk celery, thinly sliced
- ¼ teaspoon ground coriander
- ¼ teaspoon ground cumin
- salt and pepper
- 1 tablespoon olive oil
- Couscous
- ¾ cup uncooked couscous
- 1 cup vegetable broth or water
- ½ teaspoon salt (omit if using salted broth)

Directions:
1. Combine all vegetables in large bowl. Sprinkle with coriander, cumin, and salt and pepper to taste. Stir well, add olive oil, and stir again to coat vegetables evenly.

2. Place vegetables in air fryer basket and cook at 390°F for 5minutes. Stir and cook for 5 more minutes, until tender.

3. While vegetables are cooking, prepare the couscous: Place broth or water and salt in large saucepan. Heat to boiling, stir in couscous, cover, and remove from heat.

4. Let couscous sit for 5minutes, stir in cooked vegetables, and serve hot.

Rigatoni With Roasted Onions, Fennel, Spinach And Lemon Pepper Ricotta

Servings: 2
Cooking Time: 13 Minutes

Ingredients:
- 1 red onion, rough chopped into large chunks
- 2 teaspoons olive oil, divided
- 1 bulb fennel, sliced ¼-inch thick
- ¾ cup ricotta cheese
- 1½ teaspoons finely chopped lemon zest, plus more for garnish
- 1 teaspoon lemon juice
- salt and freshly ground black pepper
- 8 ounces (½ pound) dried rigatoni pasta

- 3 cups baby spinach leaves

Directions:

1. Bring a large stockpot of salted water to a boil on the stovetop and Preheat the air fryer to 400°F.

2. While the water is coming to a boil, toss the chopped onion in 1 teaspoon of olive oil and transfer to the air fryer basket. Air-fry at 400°F for 5 minutes. Toss the sliced fennel with 1 teaspoon of olive oil and add this to the air fryer basket with the onions. Continue to air-fry at 400°F for 8 minutes, shaking the basket a few times during the cooking process.

3. Combine the ricotta cheese, lemon zest and juice, ¼ teaspoon of salt and freshly ground black pepper in a bowl and stir until smooth.

4. Add the dried rigatoni to the boiling water and cook according to the package directions. When the pasta is cooked al dente, reserve one cup of the pasta water and drain the pasta into a colander.

5. Place the spinach in a serving bowl and immediately transfer the hot pasta to the bowl, wilting the spinach. Add the roasted onions and fennel and toss together. Add a little pasta water to the dish if it needs moistening. Then, dollop the lemon pepper ricotta cheese on top and nestle it into the hot pasta. Garnish with more lemon zest if desired.

Mexican Twice Air-fried Sweet Potatoes

Servings: 2
Cooking Time: 42 Minutes

Ingredients:

- 2 large sweet potatoes
- olive oil
- salt and freshly ground black pepper
- ⅓ cup diced red onion
- ⅓ cup diced red bell pepper
- ½ cup canned black beans, drained and rinsed
- ½ cup corn kernels, fresh or frozen
- ½ teaspoon chili powder
- 1½ cups grated pepper jack cheese, divided
- Jalapeño peppers, sliced

Directions:

1. Preheat the air fryer to 400°F.

2. Rub the outside of the sweet potatoes with olive oil and season with salt and freshly ground black pepper. Transfer the potatoes into the air fryer basket and air-fry at 400°F for 30 minutes, rotating the potatoes a few times during the cooking process.

3. While the potatoes are air-frying, start the potato filling. Preheat a large sauté pan over medium heat on the stovetop. Add the onion and pepper and sauté for a few minutes, until the vegetables start to soften. Add the black beans, corn, and chili powder and sauté for another 3 minutes. Set the mixture aside.

4. Remove the sweet potatoes from the air fryer and let them rest for 5 minutes. Slice off one inch of the flattest side of both potatoes. Scrape the potato flesh out of the potatoes, leaving half an inch of potato flesh around the edge of the potato. Place all the potato flesh into a large bowl and mash it with a fork. Add the black bean mixture and 1 cup of the pepper jack cheese to the mashed sweet potatoes. Season with salt and freshly ground black pepper and mix well. Stuff the hollowed out potato shells with the black bean and sweet potato mixture, mounding the filling high in the potatoes.

5. Transfer the stuffed potatoes back into the air fryer basket and air-fry at 370°F for 10 minutes.

Sprinkle the remaining cheese on top of each stuffed potato, lower the heat to 340°F and air-fry for an additional 2 minutes to melt the cheese. Top with a couple slices of Jalapeño pepper and serve warm with a green salad.

Pinto Taquitos

Servings: 4

Cooking Time: 8 Minutes

Ingredients:

- 12 corn tortillas (6- to 7-inch size)
- Filling
- ½ cup refried pinto beans
- ½ cup grated sharp Cheddar or Pepper Jack cheese
- ¼ cup corn kernels (if frozen, measure after thawing and draining)
- 2 tablespoons chopped green onion
- 2 tablespoons chopped jalapeño pepper (seeds and ribs removed before chopping)
- ½ teaspoon lime juice
- ½ teaspoon chile powder, plus extra for dusting
- ½ teaspoon cumin
- ½ teaspoon garlic powder
- oil for misting or cooking spray
- salsa, sour cream, or guacamole for dipping

Directions:

1. Mix together all filling Ingredients.

2. Warm refrigerated tortillas for easier rolling. (Wrap in damp paper towels and microwave for 30 to 60 seconds.)

3. Working with one at a time, place 1 tablespoon of filling on tortilla and roll up. Spray with oil or cooking spray and dust outside with chile powder to taste.

4. Place 6 taquitos in air fryer basket (4 on bottom layer, 2 stacked crosswise on top). Cook at 390°F for 8 minutes, until crispy and brown.

5. Repeat step 4 to cook remaining taquitos.

6. Serve plain or with salsa, sour cream, or guacamole for dipping.

Charred Cauliflower Tacos

Servings: 4

Cooking Time: 10 Minutes

Ingredients:

- 1 head cauliflower, washed and cut into florets
- 2 tablespoons avocado oil
- 2 teaspoons taco seasoning
- 1 medium avocado
- ½ teaspoon garlic powder
- ¼ teaspoon black pepper
- ¼ teaspoon salt
- 2 tablespoons chopped red onion
- 2 teaspoons fresh squeezed lime juice
- ¼ cup chopped cilantro
- Eight 6-inch corn tortillas
- ½ cup cooked corn
- ½ cup shredded purple cabbage

Directions:

1. Preheat the air fryer to 390°F.

2. In a large bowl, toss the cauliflower with the avocado oil and taco seasoning. Set the metal trivet inside the air fryer basket and liberally spray with olive oil.

3. Place the cauliflower onto the trivet and cook for 10 minutes, shaking every 3 minutes to allow for an even char.

4. While the cauliflower is cooking, prepare the avocado sauce. In a medium bowl, mash the avocado; then mix in the garlic powder, pepper, salt, and onion. Stir in the lime juice and cilantro; set aside.

5. Remove the cauliflower from the air fryer basket.

6. Place 1 tablespoon of avocado sauce in the middle of a tortilla, and top with corn, cabbage, and charred cauliflower. Repeat with the remaining tortillas. Serve immediately.

FISH AND SEAFOOD RECIPES

Italian Tuna Roast

Servings: 8
Cooking Time: 21 Minutes

Ingredients:

* cooking spray
* 1 tablespoon Italian seasoning
* ⅛ teaspoon ground black pepper
* 1 tablespoon extra-light olive oil
* 1 teaspoon lemon juice
* 1 tuna loin (approximately 2 pounds, 3 to 4 inches thick, large enough to fill a 6 x 6-inch baking dish)

Directions:

1. Spray baking dish with cooking spray and place in air fryer basket. Preheat air fryer to 390°F.
2. Mix together the Italian seasoning, pepper, oil, and lemon juice.
3. Using a dull table knife or butter knife, pierce top of tuna about every half inch: Insert knife into top of tuna roast and pierce almost all the way to the bottom.
4. Spoon oil mixture into each of the holes and use the knife to push seasonings into the tuna as deeply as possible.
5. Spread any remaining oil mixture on all outer surfaces of tuna.
6. Place tuna roast in baking dish and cook at 390°F for 20 minutes. Check temperature with a meat thermometer. Cook for an additional 1 minutes or until temperature reaches 145°F.
7. Remove basket from fryer and let tuna sit in basket for 10minutes.

Tex-mex Fish Tacos

Servings:3
Cooking Time: 7 Minutes

Ingredients:

* ¾ teaspoon Chile powder
* ¼ teaspoon Ground cumin
* ¼ teaspoon Dried oregano
* 3 5-ounce skinless mahi-mahi fillets
* Vegetable oil spray
* 3 Corn or flour tortillas
* 6 tablespoons Diced tomatoes
* 3 tablespoons Regular, low-fat, or fat-free sour cream

Directions:

1. Preheat the air fryer to 400°F.
2. Stir the chile powder, cumin, and oregano in a small bowl until well combined.
3. Coat each piece of fish all over (even the sides and ends) with vegetable oil spray. Sprinkle the spice mixture evenly over all sides of the fillets. Lightly spray them again.
4. When the machine is at temperature, set the fillets in the basket with as much air space between them as possible. Air-fry undisturbed for 7 minutes, until lightly browned and firm but not hard.
5. Use a nonstick-safe spatula to transfer the fillets to a wire rack. Microwave the tortillas on high for a few seconds, until supple. Put a fillet in each tortilla and top each with 2 tablespoons diced tomatoes and 1 tablespoon sour cream.

Lobster Tails With Lemon Garlic Butter

Servings: 2
Cooking Time: 5 Minutes

Ingredients:

- 4 ounces unsalted butter
- 1 tablespoon finely chopped lemon zest
- 1 clove garlic, thinly sliced
- 2 (6-ounce) lobster tails
- salt and freshly ground black pepper
- ½ cup white wine
- ½ lemon, sliced
- vegetable oil

Directions:

1. Start by making the lemon garlic butter. Combine the butter, lemon zest and garlic in a small saucepan. Melt and simmer the butter on the stovetop over the lowest possible heat while you prepare the lobster tails.

2. Prepare the lobster tails by cutting down the middle of the top of the shell. Crack the bottom shell by squeezing the sides of the lobster together so that you can access the lobster meat inside. Pull the lobster tail up out of the shell, but leave it attached at the base of the tail. Lay the lobster meat on top of the shell and season with salt and freshly ground black pepper. Pour a little of the lemon garlic butter on top of the lobster meat and transfer the lobster to the refrigerator so that the butter solidifies a little.

3. Pour the white wine into the air fryer drawer and add the lemon slices. Preheat the air fryer to 400°F for 5 minutes.

4. Transfer the lobster tails to the air fryer basket. Air-fry at 370° for 5 minutes, brushing more butter on halfway through cooking. (Add a minute or two if your lobster tail is more than 6-ounces.) Remove and serve with more butter for dipping or drizzling.

Garlic And Dill Salmon

Servings: 2
Cooking Time: 8 Minutes

Ingredients:

- 12 ounces salmon filets with skin
- 2 tablespoons melted butter
- 1 tablespoon extra-virgin olive oil
- 2 garlic cloves, minced
- 1 tablespoon fresh dill
- ½ teaspoon sea salt
- ½ lemon

Directions:

1. Pat the salmon dry with paper towels.
2. In a small bowl, mix together the melted butter, olive oil, garlic, and dill.
3. Sprinkle the top of the salmon with sea salt. Brush all sides of the salmon with the garlic and dill butter.
4. Preheat the air fryer to 350°F.
5. Place the salmon, skin side down, in the air fryer basket. Cook for 6 to 8 minutes, or until the fish flakes in the center.
6. Remove the salmon and plate on a serving platter. Squeeze fresh lemon over the top of the salmon. Serve immediately.

Shrimp Sliders With Avocado

Servings: 4
Cooking Time: 10 Minutes

Ingredients:

- 16 raw jumbo shrimp, peeled, deveined and tails removed (about 1 pound)
- 1 rib celery, finely chopped

- 2 carrots, grated (about ½ cup) 2 teaspoons lemon juice
- 2 teaspoons Dijon mustard
- ¼ cup chopped fresh basil or parsley
- ½ cup breadcrumbs
- ½ teaspoon salt
- freshly ground black pepper
- vegetable or olive oil, in a spray bottle
- 8 slider buns
- mayonnaise
- butter lettuce
- 2 avocados, sliced and peeled

Directions:

1. Put the shrimp into a food processor and pulse it a few times to rough chop the shrimp. Remove three quarters of the shrimp and transfer it to a bowl. Continue to process the remaining shrimp in the food processor until it is a smooth purée. Transfer the purée to the bowl with the chopped shrimp.

2. Add the celery, carrots, lemon juice, mustard, basil, breadcrumbs, salt and pepper to the bowl and combine well.

3. Preheat the air fryer to 380°F.

4. While the air fryer Preheats, shape the shrimp mixture into 8 patties. Spray both sides of the patties with oil and transfer one layer of patties to the air fryer basket. Air-fry for 10 minutes, flipping the patties over halfway through the cooking time.

5. Prepare the slider rolls by toasting them and spreading a little mayonnaise on both halves. Place a piece of butter lettuce on the bottom bun, top with the shrimp slider and then finish with the avocado slices on top. Pop the top half of the bun on top and enjoy!

Shrimp Teriyaki

Servings:10
Cooking Time: 6 Minutes

Ingredients:

- 1 tablespoon Regular or low-sodium soy sauce or gluten-free tamari sauce
- 1 tablespoon Mirin or a substitute (see here)
- 1 teaspoon Ginger juice (see the headnote)
- 10 Large shrimp (20–25 per pound), peeled and deveined
- ⅔ cup Plain panko bread crumbs (gluten-free, if a concern)
- 1 Large egg
- Vegetable oil spray

Directions:

1. Whisk the soy or tamari sauce, mirin, and ginger juice in an 8- or 9-inch square baking pan until uniform. Add the shrimp and toss well to coat. Cover and refrigerate for 1 hour, tossing the shrimp in the marinade at least twice.

2. Preheat the air fryer to 400°F.

3. Thread a marinated shrimp on a 4-inch bamboo skewer by inserting the pointy tip at the small end of the shrimp, then guiding the skewer along the shrimp so that the tip comes out the thick end and the shrimp is flat along the length of the skewer. Repeat with the remaining shrimp. (You'll need eight 4-inch skewers for the small batch, 10 skewers for the medium batch, and 12 for the large.)

4. Pour the bread crumbs onto a dinner plate. Whisk the egg in the baking pan with any marinade that stayed behind. Lay the skewers in the pan, in as close to a single layer as possible. Turn repeatedly to make sure the shrimp is coated in the egg mixture.

5. One at a time, take a skewered shrimp out of the pan and set it in the bread crumbs, turning several times and pressing gently until the shrimp is evenly coated on all sides. Coat the shrimp with vegetable oil spray and set the skewer aside. Repeat with the remainder of the shrimp.

6. Set the skewered shrimp in the basket in one layer. Air-fry undisturbed for 6 minutes, or until pink and firm.

7. Transfer the skewers to a wire rack. Cool for only a minute or two before serving.

Curried Sweet-and-spicy Scallops

Servings:3
Cooking Time: 5 Minutes

Ingredients:

- 6 tablespoons Thai sweet chili sauce
- 2 cups (from about 5 cups cereal) Crushed Rice Krispies or other rice-puff cereal
- 2 teaspoons Yellow curry powder, purchased or homemade (see here)
- 1 pound Sea scallops
- Vegetable oil spray

Directions:

1. Preheat the air fryer to 400°F.

2. Set up and fill two shallow soup plates or small pie plates on your counter: one for the chili sauce and one for crumbs, mixed with the curry powder.

3. Dip a scallop into the chili sauce, coating it on all sides. Set it in the cereal mixture and turn several times to coat evenly. Gently shake off any excess and set the scallop on a cutting board. Continue dipping and coating the remaining scallops. Coat them all on all sides with the vegetable oil spray.

4. Set the scallops in the basket with as much air space between them as possible. Air-fry undisturbed for 5 minutes, or until lightly browned and crunchy.

5. Remove the basket. Set aside for 2 minutes to let the coating set up. Then gently pour the contents of the basket onto a platter and serve at once.

Coconut Jerk Shrimp

Servings:3
Cooking Time: 8 Minutes

Ingredients:

- 1 Large egg white(s)
- 1 teaspoon Purchased or homemade jerk dried seasoning blend (see the headnote)
- ¾ cup Plain panko bread crumbs (gluten-free, if a concern)
- ¾ cup Unsweetened shredded coconut
- 12 Large shrimp (20–25 per pound), peeled and deveined
- Coconut oil spray

Directions:

1. Preheat the air fryer to 375°F .

2. Whisk the egg white(s) and seasoning blend in a bowl until foamy. Add the shrimp and toss well to coat evenly.

3. Mix the bread crumbs and coconut on a dinner plate until well combined. Use kitchen tongs to pick up a shrimp, letting the excess egg white mixture slip back into the rest. Set the shrimp in the bread-crumb mixture. Turn several times to coat evenly and thoroughly. Set on a cutting board and continue coating the remainder of the shrimp.

4. Lightly coat all the shrimp on both sides with the coconut oil spray. Set them in the basket in

one layer with as much space between them as possible. (You can even stand some up along the basket's wall in some models.) Air-fry undisturbed for 6 minutes, or until the coating is lightly browned. If the air fryer is at 360°F, you may need to add 2 minutes to the cooking time.

5. Use clean kitchen tongs to transfer the shrimp to a wire rack. Cool for only a minute or two before serving.

Bacon-wrapped Scallops

Servings: 4
Cooking Time: 8 Minutes

Ingredients:
- 16 large scallops
- 8 bacon strips
- ½ teaspoon black pepper
- ¼ teaspoon smoked paprika

Directions:
1. Pat the scallops dry with a paper towel. Slice each of the bacon strips in half. Wrap 1 bacon strip around 1 scallop and secure with a toothpick. Repeat with the remaining scallops. Season the scallops with pepper and paprika.
2. Preheat the air fryer to 350°F.
3. Place the bacon-wrapped scallops in the air fryer basket and cook for 4 minutes, shake the basket, cook another 3 minutes, shake the basket, and cook another 1 to 3 to minutes. When the bacon is crispy, the scallops should be cooked through and slightly firm, but not rubbery. Serve immediately.

Miso-rubbed Salmon Fillets

Servings:3
Cooking Time: 5 Minutes

Ingredients:

- ¼ cup White (shiro) miso paste (usually made from rice and soy beans)
- 1½ tablespoons Mirin or a substitute (see here)
- 2½ teaspoons Unseasoned rice vinegar (see here)
- Vegetable oil spray
- 3 6-ounce skin-on salmon fillets (for more information, see here)

Directions:
1. Preheat the air fryer to 400°F.
2. Mix the miso, mirin, and vinegar in a small bowl until uniform.
3. Remove the basket from the machine. Generously spray the skin side of each fillet. Pick them up one by one with a nonstick-safe spatula and set them in the basket skin side down with as much air space between them as possible. Coat the top of each fillet with the miso mixture, dividing it evenly between them.
4. Return the basket to the machine. Air-fry undisturbed for 5 minutes, or until lightly browned and firm.
5. Use a nonstick-safe spatula to transfer the fillets to serving plates. Cool for only a minute or so before serving.

Crispy Sweet-and-sour Cod Fillets

Servings:3
Cooking Time: 12 Minutes

Ingredients:
- 1½ cups Plain panko bread crumbs (gluten-free, if a concern)
- 2 tablespoons Regular or low-fat mayonnaise (not fat-free; gluten-free, if a concern)
- ¼ cup Sweet pickle relish
- 3 4- to 5-ounce skinless cod fillets

Directions:

1. Preheat the air fryer to 400°F.

2. Pour the bread crumbs into a shallow soup plate or a small pie plate. Mix the mayonnaise and relish in a small bowl until well combined. Smear this mixture all over the cod fillets. Set them in the crumbs and turn until evenly coated on all sides, even on the ends.

3. Set the coated cod fillets in the basket with as much air space between them as possible. They should not touch. Air-fry undisturbed for 12 minutes, or until browned and crisp.

4. Use a nonstick-safe spatula to transfer the cod pieces to a wire rack. Cool for only a minute or two before serving hot.

Sea Scallops

Servings: 4
Cooking Time: 8 Minutes

Ingredients:

- 1½ pounds sea scallops
- salt and pepper
- 2 eggs
- ½ cup flour
- ½ cup plain breadcrumbs
- oil for misting or cooking spray

Directions:

1. Rinse scallops and remove the tough side muscle. Sprinkle to taste with salt and pepper.

2. Beat eggs together in a shallow dish. Place flour in a second shallow dish and breadcrumbs in a third.

3. Preheat air fryer to 390°F.

4. Dip scallops in flour, then eggs, and then roll in breadcrumbs. Mist with oil or cooking spray.

5. Place scallops in air fryer basket in a single layer, leaving some space between. You should be able to cook about a dozen at a time.

6. Cook at 390°F for 8 minutes, watching carefully so as not to overcook. Scallops are done when they turn opaque all the way through. They will feel slightly firm when pressed with tines of a fork.

7. Repeat step 6 to cook remaining scallops.

Pecan-orange Crusted Striped Bass

Servings: 2
Cooking Time: 9 Minutes

Ingredients:

- flour, for dredging*
- 2 egg whites, lightly beaten
- 1 cup pecans, chopped
- 1 teaspoon finely chopped orange zest, plus more for garnish
- ½ teaspoon salt
- 2 (6-ounce) fillets striped bass
- salt and freshly ground black pepper
- vegetable or olive oil, in a spray bottle
- Orange Cream Sauce (Optional)
- ½ cup fresh orange juice
- ¼ cup heavy cream
- 1 sprig fresh thyme

Directions:

1. Set up a dredging station with three shallow dishes. Place the flour in one shallow dish. Place the beaten egg whites in a second shallow dish. Finally, combine the chopped pecans, orange zest and salt in a third shallow dish.

2. Coat the fish fillets one at a time. First season with salt and freshly ground black pepper. Then coat each fillet in flour. Shake off any excess flour

and then dip the fish into the egg white. Let the excess egg drip off and then immediately press the fish into the pecan-orange mixture. Set the crusted fish fillets aside.

3. Preheat the air fryer to 400°F.

4. Spray the crusted fish with oil and then transfer the fillets to the air fryer basket. Air-fry for 9 minutes at 400°F, flipping the fish over halfway through the cooking time. The nuts on top should be nice and toasty and the fish should feel firm to the touch.

5. If you'd like to make a sauce to go with the fish while it cooks, combine the freshly squeezed orange juice, heavy cream and sprig of thyme in a small saucepan. Simmer on the stovetop for 5 minutes and then set aside.

6. Remove the fish from the air fryer and serve over a bed of salad, like the one below. Then add a sprinkling of orange zest and a spoonful of the orange cream sauce over the top if desired.

Cajun Flounder Fillets

Servings:2
Cooking Time: 5 Minutes

Ingredients:
- 2 4-ounce skinless flounder fillet(s)
- 2 teaspoons Peanut oil
- 1 teaspoon Purchased or homemade Cajun dried seasoning blend (see the headnote)

Directions:
1. Preheat the air fryer to 400°F.
2. Oil the fillet(s) by drizzling on the peanut oil, then gently rubbing in the oil with your clean, dry fingers. Sprinkle the seasoning blend evenly over both sides of the fillet(s).
3. When the machine is at temperature, set the fillet(s) in the basket. If working with more than

one fillet, they should not touch, although they may be quite close together, depending on the basket's size. Air-fry undisturbed for 5 minutes, or until lightly browned and cooked through.

4. Use a nonstick-safe spatula to transfer the fillets to a serving platter or plate(s). Serve at once.

Lemon-roasted Salmon Fillets

Servings:3
Cooking Time: 7 Minutes

Ingredients:
- 3 6-ounce skin-on salmon fillets
- Olive oil spray
- 9 Very thin lemon slices
- ¾ teaspoon Ground black pepper
- ¼ teaspoon Table salt

Directions:
1. Preheat the air fryer to 400°F.
2. Generously coat the skin of each of the fillets with olive oil spray. Set the fillets skin side down on your work surface. Place three overlapping lemon slices down the length of each salmon fillet. Sprinkle them with the pepper and salt. Coat lightly with olive oil spray.
3. Use a nonstick-safe spatula to transfer the fillets one by one to the basket, leaving as much air space between them as possible. Air-fry undisturbed for 7 minutes, or until cooked through.
4. Use a nonstick-safe spatula to transfer the fillets to serving plates. Cool for only a minute or two before serving.

Tuna Patties With Dill Sauce

Servings: 6

Cooking Time: 10 Minutes

Ingredients:

- Two 5-ounce cans albacore tuna, drained
- ½ teaspoon garlic powder
- 2 teaspoons dried dill, divided
- ½ teaspoon black pepper
- ½ teaspoon salt, divided
- ¼ cup minced onion
- 1 large egg
- 7 tablespoons mayonnaise, divided
- ¼ cup panko breadcrumbs
- 1 teaspoon fresh lemon juice
- ¼ teaspoon fresh lemon zest
- 6 pieces butterleaf lettuce
- 1 cup diced tomatoes

Directions:

1. In a large bowl, mix the tuna with the garlic powder, 1 teaspoon of the dried dill, the black pepper, ¼ teaspoon of the salt, and the onion. Make sure to use the back of a fork to really break up the tuna so there are no large chunks.

2. Mix in the egg and 1 tablespoon of the mayonnaise; then fold in the breadcrumbs so the tuna begins to form a thick batter that holds together.

3. Portion the tuna mixture into 6 equal patties and place on a plate lined with parchment paper in the refrigerator for at least 30 minutes. This will help the patties hold together in the air fryer.

4. When ready to cook, preheat the air fryer to 350°F.

5. Liberally spray the metal trivet that sits inside the air fryer basket with olive oil mist and place the patties onto the trivet.

6. Cook for 5 minutes, flip, and cook another 5 minutes.

7. While the patties are cooking, make the dill sauce by combining the remaining 6 tablespoons of mayonnaise with the remaining 1 teaspoon of dill, the lemon juice, the lemon zest, and the remaining ¼ teaspoon of salt. Set aside.

8. Remove the patties from the air fryer.

9. Place 1 slice of lettuce on a plate and top with the tuna patty and a tomato slice. Repeat to form the remaining servings. Drizzle the dill dressing over the top. Serve immediately.

Crab Stuffed Salmon Roast

Servings: 4

Cooking Time: 20 Minutes

Ingredients:

- 1 (1½-pound) salmon fillet
- salt and freshly ground black pepper
- 6 ounces crabmeat
- 1 teaspoon finely chopped lemon zest
- 1 teaspoon Dijon mustard
- 1 tablespoon chopped fresh parsley, plus more for garnish
- 1 scallion, chopped
- ¼ teaspoon salt
- olive oil

Directions:

1. Prepare the salmon fillet by butterflying it. Slice into the thickest side of the salmon, parallel to the countertop and along the length of the fillet. Don't slice all the way through to the other side – stop about an inch from the edge. Open the salmon up like a book. Season the salmon with salt and freshly ground black pepper.

2. Make the crab filling by combining the crabmeat, lemon zest, mustard, parsley, scallion,

salt and freshly ground black pepper in a bowl. Spread this filling in the center of the salmon. Fold one side of the salmon over the filling. Then fold the other side over on top.

3. Transfer the rolled salmon to the center of a piece of parchment paper that is roughly 6- to 7-inches wide and about 12-inches long. The parchment paper will act as a sling, making it easier to put the salmon into the air fryer. Preheat the air fryer to 370°F. Use the parchment paper to transfer the salmon roast to the air fryer basket and tuck the ends of the paper down beside the salmon. Drizzle a little olive oil on top and season with salt and pepper.

4. Air-fry the salmon at 370°F for 20 minutes.

5. Remove the roast from the air fryer and let it rest for a few minutes. Then, slice it, sprinkle some more lemon zest and parsley (or fresh chives) on top and serve.

Shrimp Po'boy With Remoulade Sauce

Servings: 6
Cooking Time: 8 Minutes

Ingredients:

- ½ cup all-purpose flour
- ½ teaspoon paprika
- 1 teaspoon garlic powder
- ½ teaspoon black pepper
- ¼ teaspoon salt
- 2 eggs, whisked
- 1½ cups panko breadcrumbs
- 1 pound small shrimp, peeled and deveined
- Six 6-inch French rolls
- 2 cups shredded lettuce
- 12 ⅛-inch tomato slices
- ¾ cup Remoulade Sauce (see the following recipe)

Directions:

1. Preheat the air fryer to 360°F.

2. In a medium bowl, mix the flour, paprika, garlic powder, pepper, and salt.

3. In a shallow dish, place the eggs.

4. In a third dish, place the panko breadcrumbs.

5. Covering the shrimp in the flour, dip them into the egg, and coat them with the breadcrumbs. Repeat until all shrimp are covered in the breading.

6. Liberally spray the metal trivet that fits inside the air fryer basket with olive oil spray. Place the shrimp onto the trivet, leaving space between the shrimp to flip. Cook for 4 minutes, flip the shrimp, and cook another 4 minutes. Repeat until all the shrimp are cooked.

7. Slice the rolls in half. Stuff each roll with shredded lettuce, tomato slices, breaded shrimp, and remoulade sauce. Serve immediately.

Horseradish Crusted Salmon

Servings: 2
Cooking Time: 14 Minutes

Ingredients:

- 2 (5-ounce) salmon fillets
- salt and freshly ground black pepper
- 2 teaspoons Dijon mustard
- ½ cup panko breadcrumbs*
- 2 tablespoons prepared horseradish
- ½ teaspoon finely chopped lemon zest
- 1 tablespoon olive oil
- 1 tablespoon chopped fresh parsley

Directions:

1. Preheat the air fryer to 360°F.

2. Season the salmon with salt and freshly ground black pepper. Then spread the Dijon mustard on the salmon, coating the entire surface.

3. Combine the breadcrumbs, horseradish, lemon zest and olive oil in a small bowl. Spread the mixture over the top of the salmon and press down lightly with your hands, adhering it to the salmon using the mustard as "glue".

4. Transfer the salmon to the air fryer basket and air-fry at 360°F for 14 minutes (depending on how thick your fillet is) or until the fish feels firm to the touch. Sprinkle with the parsley.

Super Crunchy Flounder Fillets

Servings:2

Cooking Time: 6 Minutes

Ingredients:

- ½ cup All-purpose flour or tapioca flour
- 1 Large egg white(s)
- 1 tablespoon Water
- ¾ teaspoon Table salt
- 1 cup Plain panko bread crumbs (gluten-free, if a concern)
- 2 4-ounce skinless flounder fillet(s)
- Vegetable oil spray

Directions:

1. Preheat the air fryer to 400°F.

2. Set up and fill three shallow soup plates or small pie plates on your counter: one for the flour; one for the egg white(s), beaten with the water and salt until foamy; and one for the bread crumbs.

3. Dip one fillet in the flour, turning it to coat both sides. Gently shake off any excess flour, then dip the fillet in the egg white mixture, turning it to coat. Let any excess egg white mixture slip back into the rest, then set the fish in the bread crumbs. Turn it several times, gently pressing it into the crumbs to create an even crust. Generously coat both sides of the fillet with vegetable oil spray. If necessary, set it aside and continue coating the remaining fillet(s) in the same way.

4. Set the fillet(s) in the basket. If working with more than one fillet, they should not touch, although they may be quite close together, depending on the basket's size. Air-fry undisturbed for 6 minutes, or until lightly browned and crunchy.

5. Use a nonstick-safe spatula to transfer the fillet(s) to a wire rack. Cool for only a minute or two before serving.

Fish Tacos With Jalapeño-lime Sauce

Servings: 4

Cooking Time: 7 Minutes

Ingredients:

- Fish Tacos
- 1 pound fish fillets
- ¼ teaspoon cumin
- ¼ teaspoon coriander
- ⅛ teaspoon ground red pepper
- 1 tablespoon lime zest
- ¼ teaspoon smoked paprika
- 1 teaspoon oil
- cooking spray
- 6–8 corn or flour tortillas (6-inch size)
- Jalapeño-Lime Sauce
- ½ cup sour cream
- 1 tablespoon lime juice
- ¼ teaspoon grated lime zest
- ½ teaspoon minced jalapeño (flesh only)
- ¼ teaspoon cumin

- Napa Cabbage Garnish
- 1 cup shredded Napa cabbage
- ¼ cup slivered red or green bell pepper
- ¼ cup slivered onion

Directions:

1. Slice the fish fillets into strips approximately ½-inch thick.

2. Put the strips into a sealable plastic bag along with the cumin, coriander, red pepper, lime zest, smoked paprika, and oil. Massage seasonings into the fish until evenly distributed.

3. Spray air fryer basket with nonstick cooking spray and place seasoned fish inside.

4. Cook at 390°F for approximately 5minutes. Shake basket to distribute fish. Cook an additional 2 minutes, until fish flakes easily.

5. While the fish is cooking, prepare the Jalapeño-Lime Sauce by mixing the sour cream, lime juice, lime zest, jalapeño, and cumin together to make a smooth sauce. Set aside.

6. Mix the cabbage, bell pepper, and onion together and set aside.

7. To warm refrigerated tortillas, wrap in damp paper towels and microwave for 30 to 60 seconds.

8. To serve, spoon some of fish into a warm tortilla. Add one or two tablespoons Napa Cabbage Garnish and drizzle with Jalapeño-Lime Sauce.

Coconut Shrimp

Servings: 4
Cooking Time: 12 Minutes

Ingredients:

- 1 pound large shrimp (about 16 to 20), peeled and de-veined
- ½ cup flour
- salt and freshly ground black pepper
- 2 egg whites
- ½ cup fine breadcrumbs
- ½ cup shredded unsweetened coconut
- zest of one lime
- ½ teaspoon salt
- ⅛ to ¼ teaspoon ground cayenne pepper
- vegetable or canola oil
- sweet chili sauce or duck sauce (for serving)

Directions:

1. Set up a dredging station. Place the flour in a shallow dish and season well with salt and freshly ground black pepper. Whisk the egg whites in a second shallow dish. In a third shallow dish, combine the breadcrumbs, coconut, lime zest, salt and cayenne pepper.

2. Preheat the air fryer to 400°F.

3. Dredge each shrimp first in the flour, then dip it in the egg mixture, and finally press it into the breadcrumb-coconut mixture to coat all sides. Place the breaded shrimp on a plate or baking sheet and spray both sides with vegetable oil.

4. Air-fry the shrimp in two batches, being sure not to over-crowd the basket. Air-fry for 5 minutes, turning the shrimp over for the last minute or two. Repeat with the second batch of shrimp.

5. Lower the temperature of the air fryer to 340°F. Return the first batch of shrimp to the air fryer basket with the second batch and air-fry for an additional 2 minutes, just to re-heat everything.

6. Serve with sweet chili sauce, duck sauce or just eat them plain!

Crab Cakes On A Budget

Servings: 4
Cooking Time: 12 Minutes

Ingredients:

- 8 ounces imitation crabmeat
- 4 ounces leftover cooked fish (such as cod, pollock, or haddock)
- 2 tablespoons minced green onion
- 2 tablespoons minced celery
- ¾ cup crushed saltine cracker crumbs
- 2 tablespoons light mayonnaise
- 1 teaspoon prepared yellow mustard
- 1 tablespoon Worcestershire sauce, plus 2 teaspoons
- 2 teaspoons dried parsley flakes
- ½ teaspoon dried dill weed, crushed
- ½ teaspoon garlic powder
- ½ teaspoon Old Bay Seasoning
- ½ cup panko breadcrumbs
- oil for misting or cooking spray

Directions:

1. Use knives or a food processor to finely shred crabmeat and fish.
2. In a large bowl, combine all ingredients except panko and oil. Stir well.
3. Shape into 8 small, fat patties.
4. Carefully roll patties in panko crumbs to coat. Spray both sides with oil or cooking spray.
5. Place patties in air fryer basket and cook at 390°F for 12 minutes or until golden brown and crispy.

Fried Oysters

Servings:12
Cooking Time: 8 Minutes

Ingredients:

- 1½ cups All-purpose flour
- 1½ cups Yellow cornmeal
- 1½ tablespoons Cajun dried seasoning blend (for a homemade blend, see here)
- 1¼ cups, plus more if needed Amber beer, pale ale, or IPA
- 12 Large shucked oysters, any liquid drained off
- Vegetable oil spray

Directions:

1. Preheat the air fryer to 400°F.
2. Whisk ⅔ cup of the flour, ½ cup of the cornmeal, and the seasoning blend in a bowl until uniform. Set aside.
3. Whisk the remaining ⅓ cup flour and the remaining ½ cup cornmeal with the beer in a second bowl, adding more beer in dribs and drabs until the mixture is the consistency of pancake batter.
4. Using a fork, dip a shucked oyster in the beer batter, coating it thoroughly. Gently shake off any excess batter, then set the oyster in the dry mixture and turn gently to coat well and evenly. Set the coated oyster on a cutting board and continue dipping and coating the remainder of the oysters.
5. Coat the oysters with vegetable oil spray, then set them in the basket with as much air space between them as possible. Air-fry undisturbed for 8 minutes, or until lightly browned and crisp.
6. Use a nonstick-safe spatula to transfer the oysters to a wire rack. Cool for a couple of minutes before serving.

Crunchy And Buttery Cod With Ritz® Cracker Crust

Servings: 2
Cooking Time: 10 Minutes

Ingredients:

- 4 tablespoons butter, melted
- 8 to 10 RITZ® crackers, crushed into crumbs
- 2 (6-ounce) cod fillets
- salt and freshly ground black pepper
- 1 lemon

Directions:

1. Preheat the air fryer to 380°F.

2. Melt the butter in a small saucepan on the stovetop or in a microwavable dish in the microwave, and then transfer the butter to a shallow dish. Place the crushed RITZ® crackers into a second shallow dish.

3. Season the fish fillets with salt and freshly ground black pepper. Dip them into the butter and then coat both sides with the RITZ® crackers.

4. Place the fish into the air fryer basket and air-fry at 380°F for 10 minutes, flipping the fish over halfway through the cooking time.

5. Serve with a wedge of lemon to squeeze over the top.

SANDWICHES AND BURGERS RECIPES

Perfect Burgers

Servings: 3
Cooking Time: 13 Minutes

Ingredients:

*   1 pound 2 ounces 90% lean ground beef
*   1½ tablespoons Worcestershire sauce (gluten-free, if a concern)
*   ½ teaspoon Ground black pepper
*   3 Hamburger buns (gluten-free if a concern), split open

Directions:

1. Preheat the air fryer to 375°F .
2. Gently mix the ground beef, Worcestershire sauce, and pepper in a bowl until well combined but preserving as much of the meat's fibers as possible. Divide this mixture into two 5-inch patties for the small batch, three 5-inch patties for the medium, or four 5-inch patties for the large. Make a thumbprint indentation in the center of each patty, about halfway through the meat.
3. Set the patties in the basket in one layer with some space between them. Air-fry undisturbed for 10 minutes, or until an instant-read meat thermometer inserted into the center of a burger registers 160°F (a medium-well burger). You may need to add 2 minutes cooking time if the air fryer is at 360°F.
4. Use a nonstick-safe spatula, and perhaps a flatware fork for balance, to transfer the burgers to a cutting board. Set the buns cut side down in the basket in one layer (working in batches as necessary) and air-fry undisturbed for 1 minute, to toast a bit and warm up. Serve the burgers in the warm buns.

Chicken Apple Brie Melt

Servings: 3
Cooking Time: 13 Minutes

Ingredients:

*   3 5- to 6-ounce boneless skinless chicken breasts
*   Vegetable oil spray
*   1½ teaspoons Dried herbes de Provence
*   3 ounces Brie, rind removed, thinly sliced
*   6 Thin cored apple slices
*   3 French rolls (gluten-free, if a concern)
*   2 tablespoons Dijon mustard (gluten-free, if a concern)

Directions:

1. Preheat the air fryer to 375°F .
2. Lightly coat all sides of the chicken breasts with vegetable oil spray. Sprinkle the breasts evenly with the herbes de Provence.
3. When the machine is at temperature, set the breasts in the basket and air-fry undisturbed for 10 minutes.
4. Top the chicken breasts with the apple slices, then the cheese. Air-fry undisturbed for 2 minutes, or until the cheese is melty and bubbling.
5. Use a nonstick-safe spatula and kitchen tongs, for balance, to transfer the breasts to a cutting board. Set the rolls in the basket and air-fry for 1 minute to warm through. (Putting them in the machine without splitting them keeps the insides very soft while the outside gets a little crunchy.)
6. Transfer the rolls to the cutting board. Split them open lengthwise, then spread 1 teaspoon

mustard on each cut side. Set a prepared chicken breast on the bottom of a roll and close with its top, repeating as necessary to make additional sandwiches. Serve warm.

Best-ever Roast Beef Sandwiches

Servings: 6
Cooking Time: 30-50 Minutes

Ingredients:
- 2½ teaspoons Olive oil
- 1½ teaspoons Dried oregano
- 1½ teaspoons Dried thyme
- 1½ teaspoons Onion powder
- 1½ teaspoons Table salt
- 1½ teaspoons Ground black pepper
- 3 pounds Beef eye of round
- 6 Round soft rolls, such as Kaiser rolls or hamburger buns (gluten-free, if a concern), split open lengthwise
- ¾ cup Regular, low-fat, or fat-free mayonnaise (gluten-free, if a concern)
- 6 Romaine lettuce leaves, rinsed
- 6 Round tomato slices (¼ inch thick)

Directions:
1. Preheat the air fryer to 350°F .
2. Mix the oil, oregano, thyme, onion powder, salt, and pepper in a small bowl. Spread this mixture all over the eye of round.
3. When the machine is at temperature, set the beef in the basket and air-fry for 30 to 50 minutes (the range depends on the size of the cut), turning the meat twice, until an instant-read meat thermometer inserted into the thickest piece of the meat registers 130°F for rare, 140°F for medium, or 150°F for well-done.
4. Use kitchen tongs to transfer the beef to a cutting board. Cool for 10 minutes. If serving now, carve into ⅛-inch-thick slices. Spread each roll with 2 tablespoons mayonnaise and divide the beef slices between the rolls. Top with a lettuce leaf and a tomato slice and serve. Or set the beef in a container, cover, and refrigerate for up to 3 days to make cold roast beef sandwiches anytime.

Philly Cheesesteak Sandwiches

Servings: 3
Cooking Time: 9 Minutes

Ingredients:
- ¾ pound Shaved beef
- 1 tablespoon Worcestershire sauce (gluten-free, if a concern)
- ¼ teaspoon Garlic powder
- ¼ teaspoon Mild paprika
- 6 tablespoons (1½ ounces) Frozen bell pepper strips (do not thaw)
- 2 slices, broken into rings Very thin yellow or white medium onion slice(s)
- 6 ounces (6 to 8 slices) Provolone cheese slices
- 3 Long soft rolls such as hero, hoagie, or Italian sub rolls, or hot dog buns (gluten-free, if a concern), split open lengthwise

Directions:
1. Preheat the air fryer to 400°F.
2. When the machine is at temperature, spread the shaved beef in the basket, leaving a ½-inch perimeter around the meat for good air flow. Sprinkle the meat with the Worcestershire sauce, paprika, and garlic powder. Spread the peppers and onions on top of the meat.
3. Air-fry undisturbed for 6 minutes, or until cooked through. Set the cheese on top of the meat. Continue air-frying undisturbed for 3 minutes, or until the cheese has melted.

4. Use kitchen tongs to divide the meat and cheese layers in the basket between the rolls or buns. Serve hot.

Chili Cheese Dogs

Servings: 3
Cooking Time: 12 Minutes

Ingredients:
- ¾ pound Lean ground beef
- 1½ tablespoons Chile powder
- 1 cup plus 2 tablespoons Jarred sofrito
- 3 Hot dogs (gluten-free, if a concern)
- 3 Hot dog buns (gluten-free, if a concern), split open lengthwise
- 3 tablespoons Finely chopped scallion
- 9 tablespoons (a little more than 2 ounces) Shredded Cheddar cheese

Directions:
1. Crumble the ground beef into a medium or large saucepan set over medium heat. Brown well, stirring often to break up the clumps. Add the chile powder and cook for 30 seconds, stirring the whole time. Stir in the sofrito and bring to a simmer. Reduce the heat to low and simmer, stirring occasionally, for 5 minutes. Keep warm.
2. Preheat the air fryer to 400°F.
3. When the machine is at temperature, put the hot dogs in the basket and air-fry undisturbed for 10 minutes, or until the hot dogs are bubbling and blistered, even a little crisp.
4. Use kitchen tongs to put the hot dogs in the buns. Top each with a ½ cup of the ground beef mixture, 1 tablespoon of the minced scallion, and 3 tablespoons of the cheese. (The scallion should go under the cheese so it superheats and wilts a bit.) Set the filled hot dog buns in the basket and air-fry undisturbed for 2 minutes, or until the cheese has melted.
5. Remove the basket from the machine. Cool the chili cheese dogs in the basket for 5 minutes before serving.

Chicken Spiedies

Servings: 3
Cooking Time: 12 Minutes

Ingredients:
- 1¼ pounds Boneless skinless chicken thighs, trimmed of any fat blobs and cut into 2-inch pieces
- 3 tablespoons Red wine vinegar
- 2 tablespoons Olive oil
- 2 tablespoons Minced fresh mint leaves
- 2 tablespoons Minced fresh parsley leaves
- 2 teaspoons Minced fresh dill fronds
- ¾ teaspoon Fennel seeds
- ¾ teaspoon Table salt
- Up to a ¼ teaspoon Red pepper flakes
- 3 Long soft rolls, such as hero, hoagie, or Italian sub rolls (gluten-free, if a concern), split open lengthwise
- 4½ tablespoons Regular or low-fat mayonnaise (not fat-free; gluten-free, if a concern)
- 1½ tablespoons Distilled white vinegar
- 1½ teaspoons Ground black pepper

Directions:
1. Mix the chicken, vinegar, oil, mint, parsley, dill, fennel seeds, salt, and red pepper flakes in a zip-closed plastic bag. Seal, gently massage the marinade ingredients into the meat, and refrigerate for at least 2 hours or up to 6 hours. (Longer than that and the meat can turn rubbery.)

2. Set the plastic bag out on the counter (to make the contents a little less frigid). Preheat the air fryer to 400°F.

3. When the machine is at temperature, use kitchen tongs to set the chicken thighs in the basket (discard any remaining marinade) and air-fry undisturbed for 6 minutes. Turn the thighs over and continue air-frying undisturbed for 6 minutes more, until well browned, cooked through, and even a little crunchy.

4. Dump the contents of the basket onto a wire rack and cool for 2 or 3 minutes. Divide the chicken evenly between the rolls. Whisk the mayonnaise, vinegar, and black pepper in a small bowl until smooth. Drizzle this sauce over the chicken pieces in the rolls.

Thai-style Pork Sliders

Servings: 4
Cooking Time: 15 Minutes

Ingredients:

- 11 ounces Ground pork
- 2½ tablespoons Very thinly sliced scallions, white and green parts
- 4 teaspoons Minced peeled fresh ginger
- 2½ teaspoons Fish sauce (gluten-free, if a concern)
- 2 teaspoons Thai curry paste (see the headnote; gluten-free, if a concern)
- 2 teaspoons Light brown sugar
- ¾ teaspoon Ground black pepper
- 4 Slider buns (gluten-free, if a concern)

Directions:

1. Preheat the air fryer to 375°F .

2. Gently mix the pork, scallions, ginger, fish sauce, curry paste, brown sugar, and black pepper in a bowl until well combined. With clean, wet hands, form about ⅓ cup of the pork mixture into a slider about 2½ inches in diameter. Repeat until you use up all the meat—3 sliders for the small batch, 4 for the medium, and 6 for the large. (Keep wetting your hands to help the patties adhere.)

3. When the machine is at temperature, set the sliders in the basket in one layer. Air-fry undisturbed for 14 minutes, or until the sliders are golden brown and caramelized at their edges and an instant-read meat thermometer inserted into the center of a slider registers 160°F.

4. Use a nonstick-safe spatula, and perhaps a flatware fork for balance, to transfer the sliders to a cutting board. Set the buns cut side down in the basket in one layer (working in batches as necessary) and air-fry undisturbed for 1 minute, to toast a bit and warm up. Serve the sliders warm in the buns.

Thanksgiving Turkey Sandwiches

Servings: 3
Cooking Time: 10 Minutes

Ingredients:

- 1½ cups Herb-seasoned stuffing mix (not cornbread-style; gluten-free, if a concern)
- 1 Large egg white(s)
- 2 tablespoons Water
- 3 5- to 6-ounce turkey breast cutlets
- Vegetable oil spray
- 4½ tablespoons Purchased cranberry sauce, preferably whole berry
- ⅛ teaspoon Ground cinnamon
- ⅛ teaspoon Ground dried ginger
- 4½ tablespoons Regular, low-fat, or fat-free mayonnaise (gluten-free, if a concern)
- 6 tablespoons Shredded Brussels sprouts

- 3 Kaiser rolls (gluten-free, if a concern), split open

Directions:

1. Preheat the air fryer to 375°F .

2. Put the stuffing mix in a heavy zip-closed bag, seal it, lay it flat on your counter, and roll a rolling pin over the bag to crush the stuffing mix to the consistency of rough sand. (Or you can pulse the stuffing mix to the desired consistency in a food processor.)

3. Set up and fill two shallow soup plates or small pie plates on your counter: one for the egg white(s), whisked with the water until foamy; and one for the ground stuffing mix.

4. Dip a cutlet in the egg white mixture, coating both sides and letting any excess egg white slip back into the rest. Set the cutlet in the ground stuffing mix and coat it evenly on both sides, pressing gently to coat well on both sides. Lightly coat the cutlet on both sides with vegetable oil spray, set it aside, and continue dipping and coating the remaining cutlets in the same way.

5. Set the cutlets in the basket and air-fry undisturbed for 10 minutes, or until crisp and brown. Use kitchen tongs to transfer the cutlets to a wire rack to cool for a few minutes.

6. Meanwhile, stir the cranberry sauce with the cinnamon and ginger in a small bowl. Mix the shredded Brussels sprouts and mayonnaise in a second bowl until the vegetable is evenly coated.

7. Build the sandwiches by spreading about 1½ tablespoons of the cranberry mixture on the cut side of the bottom half of each roll. Set a cutlet on top, then spread about 3 tablespoons of the Brussels sprouts mixture evenly over the cutlet. Set the other half of the roll on top and serve warm.

Mexican Cheeseburgers

Servings: 4
Cooking Time: 22 Minutes

Ingredients:

- 1¼ pounds ground beef
- ¼ cup finely chopped onion
- ½ cup crushed yellow corn tortilla chips
- 1 (1.25-ounce) packet taco seasoning
- ¼ cup canned diced green chilies
- 1 egg, lightly beaten
- 4 ounces pepper jack cheese, grated
- 4 (12-inch) flour tortillas
- shredded lettuce, sour cream, guacamole, salsa (for topping)

Directions:

1. Combine the ground beef, minced onion, crushed tortilla chips, taco seasoning, green chilies, and egg in a large bowl. Mix thoroughly until combined – your hands are good tools for this. Divide the meat into four equal portions and shape each portion into an oval-shaped burger.

2. Preheat the air fryer to 370°F.

3. Air-fry the burgers for 18 minutes, turning them over halfway through the cooking time. Divide the cheese between the burgers, lower fryer to 340°F and air-fry for an additional 4 minutes to melt the cheese. (This will give you a burger that is medium-well. If you prefer your cheeseburger medium-rare, shorten the cooking time to about 15 minutes and then add the cheese and proceed with the recipe.)

4. While the burgers are cooking, warm the tortillas wrapped in aluminum foil in a 350°F oven, or in a skillet with a little oil over medium-high heat for a couple of minutes. Keep the tortillas warm until the burgers are ready.

5. To assemble the burgers, spread sour cream over three quarters of the tortillas and top each with some shredded lettuce and salsa. Place the Mexican cheeseburgers on the lettuce and top with guacamole. Fold the tortillas around the burger, starting with the bottom and then folding the sides in over the top. (A little sour cream can help hold the seam of the tortilla together.) Serve immediately.

White Bean Veggie Burgers

Servings: 3
Cooking Time: 13 Minutes

Ingredients:
- 1⅓ cups Drained and rinsed canned white beans
- 3 tablespoons Rolled oats (not quick-cooking or steel-cut; gluten-free, if a concern)
- 3 tablespoons Chopped walnuts
- 2 teaspoons Olive oil
- 2 teaspoons Lemon juice
- 1½ teaspoons Dijon mustard (gluten-free, if a concern)
- ¾ teaspoon Dried sage leaves
- ¼ teaspoon Table salt
- Olive oil spray
- 3 Whole-wheat buns or gluten-free whole-grain buns (if a concern), split open

Directions:
1. Preheat the air fryer to 400°F.
2. Place the beans, oats, walnuts, oil, lemon juice, mustard, sage, and salt in a food processor. Cover and process to make a coarse paste that will hold its shape, about like wet sugar-cookie dough, stopping the machine to scrape down the inside of the canister at least once.

3. Scrape down and remove the blade. With clean and wet hands, form the bean paste into two 4-inch patties for the small batch, three 4-inch patties for the medium, or four 4-inch patties for the large batch. Generously coat the patties on both sides with olive oil spray.
4. Set them in the basket with some space between them and air-fry undisturbed for 12 minutes, or until lightly brown and crisp at the edges. The tops of the burgers will feel firm to the touch.
5. Use a nonstick-safe spatula, and perhaps a flatware fork for balance, to transfer the burgers to a cutting board. Set the buns cut side down in the basket in one layer (working in batches as necessary) and air-fry undisturbed for 1 minute, to toast a bit and warm up. Serve the burgers warm in the buns.

Chicken Saltimbocca Sandwiches

Servings: 3
Cooking Time: 11 Minutes

Ingredients:
- 3 5- to 6-ounce boneless skinless chicken breasts
- 6 Thin prosciutto slices
- 6 Provolone cheese slices
- 3 Long soft rolls, such as hero, hoagie, or Italian sub rolls (gluten-free, if a concern), split open lengthwise
- 3 tablespoons Pesto, purchased or homemade (see the headnote)

Directions:
1. Preheat the air fryer to 400°F.
2. Wrap each chicken breast with 2 prosciutto slices, spiraling the prosciutto around the breast and overlapping the slices a bit to cover the breast.

The prosciutto will stick to the chicken more readily than bacon does.

3. When the machine is at temperature, set the wrapped chicken breasts in the basket and air-fry undisturbed for 10 minutes, or until the prosciutto is frizzled and the chicken is cooked through.

4. Overlap 2 cheese slices on each breast. Air-fry undisturbed for 1 minute, or until melted. Take the basket out of the machine.

5. Smear the insides of the rolls with the pesto, then use kitchen tongs to put a wrapped and cheesy chicken breast in each roll.

Dijon Thyme Burgers

Servings: 3

Cooking Time: 18 Minutes

Ingredients:

- 1 pound lean ground beef
- ⅓ cup panko breadcrumbs
- ¼ cup finely chopped onion
- 3 tablespoons Dijon mustard
- 1 tablespoon chopped fresh thyme
- 4 teaspoons Worcestershire sauce
- 1 teaspoon salt
- freshly ground black pepper
- Topping (optional):
- 2 tablespoons Dijon mustard
- 1 tablespoon dark brown sugar
- 1 teaspoon Worcestershire sauce
- 4 ounces sliced Swiss cheese, optional

Directions:

1. Combine all the burger ingredients together in a large bowl and mix well. Divide the meat into 4 equal portions and then form the burgers, being careful not to over-handle the meat. One good way to do this is to throw the meat back and forth from one hand to another, packing the meat each time you catch it. Flatten the balls into patties, making an indentation in the center of each patty with your thumb (this will help it stay flat as it cooks) and flattening the sides of the burgers so that they will fit nicely into the air fryer basket.

2. Preheat the air fryer to 370°F.

3. If you don't have room for all four burgers, air-fry two or three burgers at a time for 8 minutes. Flip the burgers over and air-fry for another 6 minutes.

4. While the burgers are cooking combine the Dijon mustard, dark brown sugar, and Worcestershire sauce in a small bowl and mix well. This optional topping to the burgers really adds a boost of flavor at the end. Spread the Dijon topping evenly on each burger. If you cooked the burgers in batches, return the first batch to the cooker at this time – it's ok to place the fourth burger on top of the others in the center of the basket. Air-fry the burgers for another 3 minutes.

5. Finally, if desired, top each burger with a slice of Swiss cheese. Lower the air fryer temperature to 330°F and air-fry for another minute to melt the cheese. Serve the burgers on toasted brioche buns, dressed the way you like them.

Crunchy Falafel Balls

Servings: 8
Cooking Time: 16 Minutes

Ingredients:

- 2½ cups Drained and rinsed canned chickpeas
- ¼ cup Olive oil
- 3 tablespoons All-purpose flour
- 1½ teaspoons Dried oregano
- 1½ teaspoons Dried sage leaves
- 1½ teaspoons Dried thyme
- ¾ teaspoon Table salt
- Olive oil spray

Directions:

1. Preheat the air fryer to 400°F.
2. Place the chickpeas, olive oil, flour, oregano, sage, thyme, and salt in a food processor. Cover and process into a paste, stopping the machine at least once to scrape down the inside of the canister.
3. Scrape down and remove the blade. Using clean, wet hands, form 2 tablespoons of the paste into a ball, then continue making 9 more balls for a small batch, 15 more for a medium one, and 19 more for a large batch. Generously coat the balls in olive oil spray.
4. Set the balls in the basket in one layer with a little space between them and air-fry undisturbed for 16 minutes, or until well browned and crisp.
5. Dump the contents of the basket onto a wire rack. Cool for 5 minutes before serving.

Inside-out Cheeseburgers

Servings: 3
Cooking Time: 9-11 Minutes

Ingredients:

- 1 pound 2 ounces 90% lean ground beef
- ¾ teaspoon Dried oregano
- ¾ teaspoon Table salt
- ¾ teaspoon Ground black pepper
- ¼ teaspoon Garlic powder
- 6 tablespoons (about 1½ ounces) Shredded Cheddar, Swiss, or other semi-firm cheese, or a purchased blend of shredded cheeses
- 3 Hamburger buns (gluten-free, if a concern), split open

Directions:

1. Preheat the air fryer to 375°F .
2. Gently mix the ground beef, oregano, salt, pepper, and garlic powder in a bowl until well combined without turning the mixture to mush. Form it into two 6-inch patties for the small batch, three for the medium, or four for the large.
3. Place 2 tablespoons of the shredded cheese in the center of each patty. With clean hands, fold the sides of the patty up to cover the cheese, then pick it up and roll it gently into a ball to seal the cheese inside. Gently press it back into a 5-inch burger without letting any cheese squish out. Continue filling and preparing more burgers, as needed.
4. Place the burgers in the basket in one layer and air-fry undisturbed for 8 minutes for medium or 10 minutes for well-done. (An instant-read meat thermometer won't work for these burgers because it will hit the mostly melted cheese inside and offer a hotter temperature than the surrounding meat.)
5. Use a nonstick-safe spatula, and perhaps a flatware fork for balance, to transfer the burgers to a cutting board. Set the buns cut side down in the basket in one layer (working in batches as necessary) and air-fry undisturbed for 1 minute, to toast a bit and warm up. Cool the burgers a few minutes more, then serve them warm in the buns.

Black Bean Veggie Burgers

Servings: 3

Cooking Time: 10 Minutes

Ingredients:

- 1 cup Drained and rinsed canned black beans
- ⅓ cup Pecan pieces
- ⅓ cup Rolled oats (not quick-cooking or steel-cut; gluten-free, if a concern)
- 2 tablespoons (or 1 small egg) Pasteurized egg substitute, such as Egg Beaters (gluten-free, if a concern)
- 2 teaspoons Red ketchup-like chili sauce, such as Heinz
- ¼ teaspoon Ground cumin
- ¼ teaspoon Dried oregano
- ¼ teaspoon Table salt
- ¼ teaspoon Ground black pepper
- Olive oil
- Olive oil spray

Directions:

1. Preheat the air fryer to 400°F.

2. Put the beans, pecans, oats, egg substitute or egg, chili sauce, cumin, oregano, salt, and pepper in a food processor. Cover and process to a coarse paste that will hold its shape like sugar-cookie dough, adding olive oil in 1-teaspoon increments to get the mixture to blend smoothly. The amount of olive oil is actually dependent on the internal moisture content of the beans and the oats. Figure on about 1 tablespoon (three 1-teaspoon additions) for the smaller batch, with proportional increases for the other batches. A little too much olive oil can't hurt, but a dry paste will fall apart as it cooks and a far-too-wet paste will stick to the basket.

3. Scrape down and remove the blade. Using clean, wet hands, form the paste into two 4-inch patties for the small batch, three 4-inch patties for the medium, or four 4-inch patties for the large batch, setting them one by one on a cutting board. Generously coat both sides of the patties with olive oil spray.

4. Set them in the basket in one layer. Air-fry undisturbed for 10 minutes, or until lightly browned and crisp at the edges.

5. Use a nonstick-safe spatula, and perhaps a flatware fork for balance, to transfer the burgers to a wire rack. Cool for 5 minutes before serving.

Chicken Club Sandwiches

Servings: 3

Cooking Time: 15 Minutes

Ingredients:

- 3 5- to 6-ounce boneless skinless chicken breasts
- 6 Thick-cut bacon strips (gluten-free, if a concern)
- 3 Long soft rolls, such as hero, hoagie, or Italian sub rolls (gluten-free, if a concern)
- 3 tablespoons Regular, low-fat, or fat-free mayonnaise (gluten-free, if a concern)
- 3 Lettuce leaves, preferably romaine or iceberg
- 6 ¼-inch-thick tomato slices

Directions:

1. Preheat the air fryer to 375°F .

2. Wrap each chicken breast with 2 strips of bacon, spiraling the bacon around the meat, slightly overlapping the strips on each revolution. Start the second strip of bacon farther down the breast but on a line with the start of the first strip so they both end at a lined-up point on the chicken breast.

3. When the machine is at temperature, set the wrapped breasts bacon-seam side down in the basket with space between them. Air-fry undisturbed for 12 minutes, until the bacon is browned, crisp, and cooked through and an instant-read meat thermometer inserted into the center of a breast registers 165°F. You may need to add 2 minutes in the air fryer if the temperature is at 360°F.

4. Use kitchen tongs to transfer the breasts to a wire rack. Split the rolls open lengthwise and set them cut side down in the basket. Air-fry for 1 minute, or until warmed through.

5. Use kitchen tongs to transfer the rolls to a cutting board. Spread 1 tablespoon mayonnaise on the cut side of one half of each roll. Top with a chicken breast, lettuce leaf, and tomato slice. Serve warm.

Lamb Burgers

Servings: 3
Cooking Time: 17 Minutes

Ingredients:
- 1 pound 2 ounces Ground lamb
- 3 tablespoons Crumbled feta
- 1 teaspoon Minced garlic
- 1 teaspoon Tomato paste
- ¾ teaspoon Ground coriander
- ¾ teaspoon Ground dried ginger
- Up to ⅛ teaspoon Cayenne
- Up to a ⅛ teaspoon Table salt (optional)
- 3 Kaiser rolls or hamburger buns (gluten-free, if a concern), split open

Directions:
1. Preheat the air fryer to 375°F .
2. Gently mix the ground lamb, feta, garlic, tomato paste, coriander, ginger, cayenne, and salt (if using) in a bowl until well combined, trying to keep the bits of cheese intact. Form this mixture into two 5-inch patties for the small batch, three 5-inch patties for the medium, or four 5-inch patties for the large.

3. Set the patties in the basket in one layer and air-fry undisturbed for 16 minutes, or until an instant-read meat thermometer inserted into one burger registers 160°F. (The cheese is not an issue with the temperature probe in this recipe as it was for the Inside-Out Cheeseburgers, because the feta is so well mixed into the ground meat.)

4. Use a nonstick-safe spatula, and perhaps a flatware fork for balance, to transfer the burgers to a cutting board. Set the buns cut side down in the basket in one layer (working in batches as necessary) and air-fry undisturbed for 1 minute, to toast a bit and warm up. Serve the burgers warm in the buns.

Salmon Burgers

Servings: 3
Cooking Time: 8 Minutes

Ingredients:
- 1 pound 2 ounces Skinless salmon fillet, preferably fattier Atlantic salmon
- 1½ tablespoons Minced chives or the green part of a scallion
- ½ cup Plain panko bread crumbs (gluten-free, if a concern)
- 1½ teaspoons Dijon mustard (gluten-free, if a concern)
- 1½ teaspoons Drained and rinsed capers, minced
- 1½ teaspoons Lemon juice
- ¼ teaspoon Table salt
- ¼ teaspoon Ground black pepper

- Vegetable oil spray

Directions:

1. Preheat the air fryer to 375°F .

2. Cut the salmon into pieces that will fit in a food processor. Cover and pulse until coarsely chopped. Add the chives and pulse to combine, until the fish is ground but not a paste. Scrape down and remove the blade. Scrape the salmon mixture into a bowl. Add the bread crumbs, mustard, capers, lemon juice, salt, and pepper. Stir gently until well combined.

3. Use clean and dry hands to form the mixture into two 5-inch patties for a small batch, three 5-inch patties for a medium batch, or four 5-inch patties for a large one.

4. Coat both sides of each patty with vegetable oil spray. Set them in the basket in one layer and air-fry undisturbed for 8 minutes, or until browned and an instant-read meat thermometer inserted into the center of a burger registers 145°F.

5. Use a nonstick-safe spatula, and perhaps a flatware fork for balance, to transfer the burgers to a wire rack. Cool for 2 or 3 minutes before serving.

Provolone Stuffed Meatballs

Servings: 4

Cooking Time: 12 Minutes

Ingredients:

- 1 tablespoon olive oil
- 1 small onion, very finely chopped
- 1 to 2 cloves garlic, minced
- ¾ pound ground beef
- ¾ pound ground pork
- ¾ cup breadcrumbs
- ¼ cup grated Parmesan cheese
- ¼ cup finely chopped fresh parsley (or 1 tablespoon dried parsley)
- ½ teaspoon dried oregano
- 1½ teaspoons salt
- freshly ground black pepper
- 2 eggs, lightly beaten
- 5 ounces sharp or aged provolone cheese, cut into 1-inch cubes

Directions:

1. Preheat a skillet over medium-high heat. Add the oil and cook the onion and garlic until tender, but not browned.

2. Transfer the onion and garlic to a large bowl and add the beef, pork, breadcrumbs, Parmesan cheese, parsley, oregano, salt, pepper and eggs. Mix well until all the ingredients are combined. Divide the mixture into 12 evenly sized balls. Make one meatball at a time, by pressing a hole in the meatball mixture with your finger and pushing a piece of provolone cheese into the hole. Mold the meat back into a ball, enclosing the cheese.

3. Preheat the air fryer to 380°F.

4. Working in two batches, transfer six of the meatballs to the air fryer basket and air-fry for 12 minutes, shaking the basket and turning the meatballs a couple of times during the cooking process. Repeat with the remaining six meatballs. You can pop the first batch of meatballs into the air fryer for the last two minutes of cooking to re-heat them. Serve warm.

Asian Glazed Meatballs

Servings: 4

Cooking Time: 10 Minutes

Ingredients:

- 1 large shallot, finely chopped
- 2 cloves garlic, minced
- 1 tablespoon grated fresh ginger
- 2 teaspoons fresh thyme, finely chopped
- 1½ cups brown mushrooms, very finely chopped (a food processor works well here)
- 2 tablespoons soy sauce
- freshly ground black pepper
- 1 pound ground beef
- ½ pound ground pork
- 3 egg yolks
- 1 cup Thai sweet chili sauce (spring roll sauce)
- ¼ cup toasted sesame seeds
- 2 scallions, sliced

Directions:

1. Combine the shallot, garlic, ginger, thyme, mushrooms, soy sauce, freshly ground black pepper, ground beef and pork, and egg yolks in a bowl and mix the ingredients together. Gently shape the mixture into 24 balls, about the size of a golf ball.

2. Preheat the air fryer to 380°F.

3. Working in batches, air-fry the meatballs for 8 minutes, turning the meatballs over halfway through the cooking time. Drizzle some of the Thai sweet chili sauce on top of each meatball and return the basket to the air fryer, air-frying for another 2 minutes. Reserve the remaining Thai sweet chili sauce for serving.

4. As soon as the meatballs are done, sprinkle with toasted sesame seeds and transfer them to a serving platter. Scatter the scallions around and serve warm.

RECIPE INDEX

Printed by Libri Plureos GmbH in Hamburg, Germany